TUSCANY

ROAD TRIPS

This edition written and researched by

**Duncan Garwood, Paula Hardy,
Robert Landon and Nicola Williams**

HOW TO USE THIS BOOK

Reviews

In the Destinations section:

All reviews are ordered in our authors' preference, starting with their most preferred option. Additionally:

Sights are arranged in the geographic order that we suggest you visit them and, within this order, by author preference.

Eating and Sleeping reviews are ordered by price range (budget, midrange, top end) and, within these ranges, by author preference.

Map Legend

Routes
- Trip Route
- Trip Detour
- Linked Trip
- Walk Route
- Tollway
- Freeway
- Primary
- Secondary
- Tertiary
- Lane
- Unsealed Road
- Plaza/Mall
- Steps
- Tunnel
- Pedestrian Overpass
- Walk Track/Path

Boundaries
- International
- State/Province
- Cliff

Hydrography
- River/Creek
- Intermittent River
- Swamp/Mangrove
- Canal
- Water
- Dry/Salt/Intermittent Lake
- Glacier

Highway Markers
- A6 Autostrada
- SS231 State Highway
- SR203 Regional Highway
- SP3 Provincial Highway
- E74 Other Road

Trips
- 1 Trip Numbers
- 9 Trip Stop
- Walking tour
- Trip Detour

Population
- Capital (National)
- Capital (State/Province)
- City/Large Town
- Town/Village

Areas
- Beach
- Cemetery (Christian)
- Cemetery (Other)
- Park
- Forest
- Reservation
- Urban Area
- Sportsground

Transport
- Airport
- Cable Car/Funicular
- Metro station
- Parking
- Train/Railway
- Tram

Note: Not all symbols displayed above appear on the maps in this book

Symbols In This Book

- ✓ Top Tips
- 🍷 Food & Drink
- 🔗 Link Your Trips
- 🌳 Outdoors
- 💡 Tips from Locals
- 📷 Essential Photo
- ➡ Trip Detour
- 🏃 Walking Tour
- 📖 History & Culture
- 🍴 Eating
- 👨‍👩‍👧 Family
- 🛏 Sleeping

- 👁 Sights
- 🛏 Sleeping
- 🏖 Beaches
- 🍴 Eating
- 🏃 Activities
- 🍷 Drinking
- 🎓 Courses
- ☆ Entertainment
- ☞ Tours
- 🛍 Shopping
- 🎆 Festivals & Events
- ℹ Information & Transport

These symbols and abbreviations give vital information for each listing:

- 📞 Telephone number
- 🐾 Pet-friendly
- 🕙 Opening hours
- 🚌 Bus
- 🅿 Parking
- 🚢 Ferry
- 🚭 Nonsmoking
- 🚊 Tram
- ❄ Air-conditioning
- 🚆 Train
- @ Internet access
- apt apartments
- 🛜 Wi-fi access
- d double rooms
- 🏊 Swimming pool
- dm dorm beds
- 🥗 Vegetarian selection
- q quad rooms
- r rooms
- 📖 English-language menu
- s single rooms
- ste suites
- 👪 Family-friendly
- tr triple rooms
- tw twin rooms

CONTENTS

Murals in a medieval village near Bologna

WELCOME TO
TUSCANY

As Florence's Renaissance skyline fades into the background, the open road beckons. Motoring through Tuscany's voluptuous, wine-rich hills is one of Italy's great driving experiences – and one of the many on offer in this fascinating part of the country.

When people imagine classic Tuscan countryside, they usually conjure up images of central Tuscany. However, there's more to this popular region than rolling hills, sun-kissed vineyards and avenues of cypress trees. The real gems are the historic towns and cities, most of which are medieval and Renaissance time capsules magically transported to the modern day.

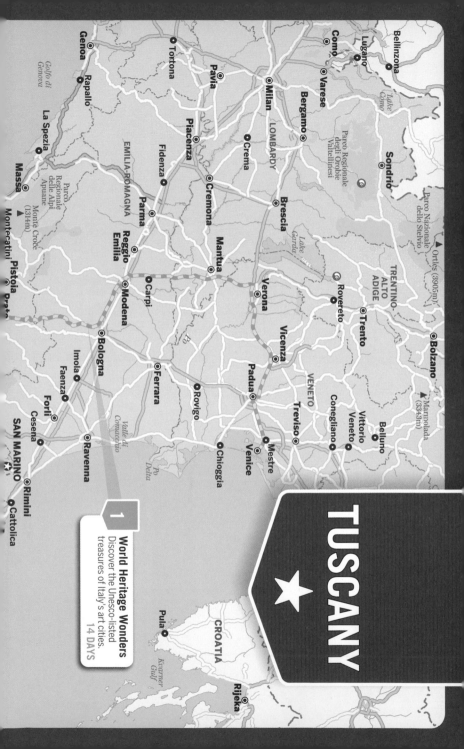

TUSCANY ★

1
World Heritage Wonders
Discover the Unesco-listed
treasures of Italy's art cities.
14 DAYS

Genoa

Golfo di
Genova

Rapallo

La Spezia

Massa

Montecatini
Pistoia
Prato

Parco
Regionale
delle Alpi
Apuane

Monte Croce
(1314m)

Tortona

Pavia

Piacenza

Fidenza

EMILIA-ROMAGNA

Parma

Reggio
Emilia

Modena

Carpi

Bologna

Imola

Faenza

Forlì

Cesena

Ravenna

SAN MARINO

Rimini

Cattolica

Como

Lugano

Bellinzona

Varese

Milan

Bergamo

LOMBARDY

Crema

Cremona

Brescia

Mantua

Verona

Vicenza

Padua

Ferrara

Rovigo

Chioggia

Venice

Mestre

Treviso

Conegliano

Belluno

Vittorio
Veneto

VENETO

Valle di
Comacchio

Po
Delta

Sondrio

Parco Regionale
degli Orobie
Valtellinesi

Lake
Como

Parco Nazionale
dello Stelvio

Ortles (3905m)

Rovereto

Trento

TRENTINO-
ALTO
ADIGE

Bolzano

Marmolada
(3343m)

Lake
Garda

Pula

CROATIA

Kvarner
Gulf

Rijeka

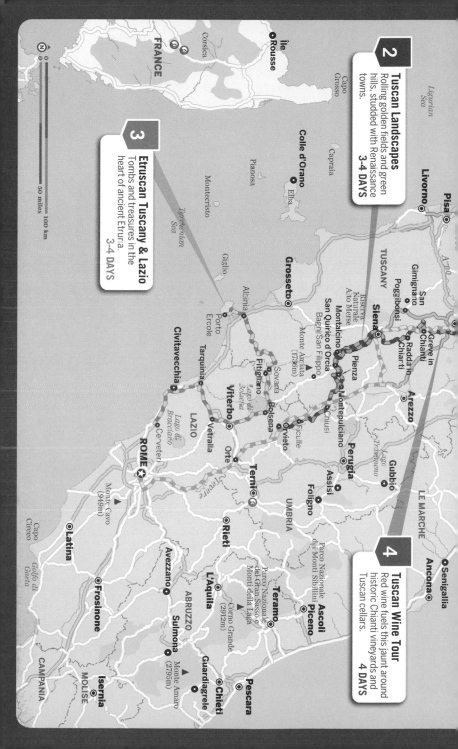

TUSCANY
HIGHLIGHTS
★

Montalcino (above) Taste some of Italy's great wines and enjoy the provincial pace of this pretty hillside town. See it on Trip 4

Siena (left) An enchanting, beautifully preserved medieval city. See it on Trips 2 & 4

Cerveteri (right) Elaborate Etruscan tombs make up a veritable town of the dead. See it on Trip 3

MICHELE ALFIERI/SHUTTERSTOCK ©

CITY GUIDE

FLORENCE

An essential stop on every Italian itinerary, Florence (Firenze) is one of the world's great art cities, boasting Renaissance icons and a wonderfully intact *centro storico* (historic centre). Beyond the Michelangelo masterpieces and Medici *palazzi* (mansions), there's a buzzing bar scene and great shopping in artisan workshops and designer boutiques.

Getting Around

Non-resident traffic is banned from the centre of Florence for most of the week, and if you enter the Limited Traffic Zone (ZTL) you risk a €150 fine. Rather than drive, walk or use the city buses; tickets cost €1.20 prebought or €2 on board.

Parking

There is free parking around Piazzale Michelangelo (park within the blue lines). Pricey (around €20 per day) underground parking can be found around Fortezza da Basso and in the Oltrarno beneath Piazzale di Porta Romana. Otherwise, ask if your hotel can arrange parking.

Ponte Vecchio (p61) and the Arno river

Discover the Taste of Florence

Florence teems with restaurants, trattorias, *osterie* (casual taverns) and wine bars catering to all budgets. Top neighbourhoods include Santa Croce, home to some of the city's best restaurants, and over-the-river Oltrarno.

Live Like a Local

To be right in the heart of it, go for the Duomo and Piazza della Signoria areas, which have some excellent budget options. Near the train station, Santa Maria Novella has some good midrange boutique/design hotels.

Useful Websites

Firenze Turismo (www.firenzeturismo.it) Official tourist site; comprehensive and up to date.

The Florentine (www.theflorentine.com) For accommodation, information and practical advice.

Firenze Musei (www.firenzemusei.it) Book tickets for the Uffizi and Accademia museums.

Trips through Florence: 1 4

Destination Coverage: p56

ROME

Even in a country of exquisite cities, Rome (Roma) is special. Pulsating, seductive and utterly disarming, it's a mesmerising mix of artistic masterpieces and iconic monuments, theatrical piazzas and haunting ruins. If your road leads to Rome, give yourself a couple of days to explore its headline sights.

Getting Around

Driving is not the best way to get around Rome. Traffic can be chaotic and much of the *centro storico* is closed to nonauthorised traffic on weekdays and weekend evenings. You're better off using public transport; a day pass is €6.

Parking

On-street parking, which is expensive and scarce, is denoted by blue lines. There are a few car parks in the centre, which charge about €15 to €20 per day. Some top-end hotels offer parking, usually for an extra charge.

Spiral staircase, Vatican Museums (p100)

TOP EXPERIENCES

➡ Get to the Heart of the Ancient City
Thrill to the sight of the Colosseum, Roman Forum and Palatino, where Romulus and Remus supposedly founded the city in 753 BC.

➡ Gaze Heavenwards in the Sistine Chapel
File past kilometres of priceless art at the Vatican Museums to arrive at the Sistine Chapel and Michelangelo's fabled frescoes. (www.vatican.va)

➡ Villa Borghese's Baroque Treasures
Head to the Museo e Galleria Borghese to marvel at a series of exhilarating sculptures by baroque maestro Gian Lorenzo Bernini. (www.galleriaborghese.it)

➡ Admire the Pantheon's Dome
The Pantheon is the best preserved of Rome's ancient monuments, but it's only when you get inside that you get the full measure of the place as its dome soars above you.

Discover the Taste of Rome
For authentic nose-to-tail Roman cooking check out the trattorias in Testaccio, and for traditional Roman-Jewish cuisine head to the atmospheric Jewish Ghetto.

Live Like a Local
The most atmospheric, and expensive, place to stay is the *centro storico*, where you'll have everything on your doorstep. Night owls will enjoy Trastevere, while Tridente offers refined accommodation and designer shopping. The Vatican area is also popular.

Useful Websites
060608 (www.060608.it) Official tourist website.

Pierreci (www.pierreci.it) Information and ticket booking for Rome's monuments.

Lonely Planet (www.lonelyplanet.com/rome) Destination low-down, hotels and traveller forum.

Trips through Rome: 1

Destination Coverage: p98

NEED TO KNOW

CURRENCY
Euro (€)

LANGUAGE
Italian

VISAS
Generally not required for stays of up to 90 days (or at all for EU nationals); some nationalities need a Schengen visa (p128).

FUEL
You'll find filling stations on autostradas and all major roads. The price of fuel can be higher in Italy than in neighbouring countries; be sure to check before you go.

RENTAL CARS
Avis (www.avis.com)

Europcar (www.europcar.com)

Hertz (www.hertz.com)

Maggiore (www.maggiore.it)

IMPORTANT NUMBERS
Ambulance (☏118)

Emergency (☏112)

Police (☏113)

Roadside Assistance (☏803 116; ☏800 116800 from a foreign mobile phone)

Climate

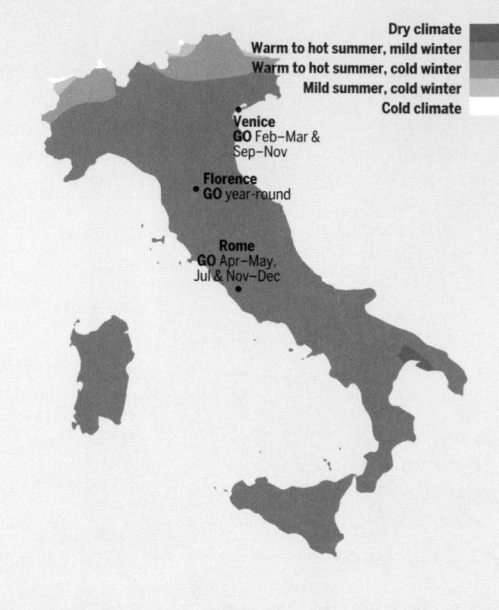

Dry climate
Warm to hot summer, mild winter
Warm to hot summer, cold winter
Mild summer, cold winter
Cold climate

Venice
GO Feb–Mar & Sep–Nov

Florence
GO year-round

Rome
GO Apr–May, Jul & Nov–Dec

When to Go

High Season (generally Jul–Aug)
» Prices high on the coast; accommodation discounts available in some cities in August.

» Prices rocket for Christmas, New Year and Easter.

» Late December to March is high season in the Alps and Dolomites.

Shoulder Season (Apr–Jun & Sep–Oct)
» Good deals on accommodation, especially in the south.

» Spring is best for festivals, flowers and local produce.

» Autumn provides warm weather and the grape harvest.

Low Season (Nov–Mar)
» Prices at their lowest – up to 30% less than in high season.

» Many sights and hotels closed in coastal and mountainous areas.

» A good period for cultural events in large cities.

Daily Costs

Budget: Less than €100

» Double room in a budget hotel: €50–€100

» Pizza or pasta: €6–€12

» Excellent markets and delis for self-catering

Midrange: €100–€200

» Double room in a midrange hotel: €80–€180

» Lunch and dinner in local restaurants: €25–€45

» Museum admission: €5–€15

Top End: More than €200

» Double room in a four- or five-star hotel: €200–€450

» Top-restaurant dinner: €50–€150

» Opera tickets: €15–€150

Eating

Restaurants (Ristoranti) Formal service and refined dishes, with prices to match.

Trattorias Family-run places with informal service and classic regional cooking.

Vegetarians Most places offer good vegetable starters and side dishes.

Price indicators for a meal with *primo* (first course), *secondo* (second course), a glass of house wine and *coperto* (cover charge):

€	less than €25
€€	€25–€45
€€€	more than €45

Sleeping

Hotels From luxury boutique palaces to modest family-run *pensioni* (small hotels).

B&Bs Rooms in restored farmhouses, city *palazzi* (mansions) or seaside bungalows.

Agriturismi Farmstays range from working farms to luxury rural retreats.

Price indicators for a double room with bathroom and breakfast included:

€	less than €110
€€	€110–€200
€€€	more than €200

Arriving in Italy

Leonardo da Vinci (Fiumicino) Airport (Rome)

Rental cars Agencies are near the multilevel car park. Look for signs in the Arrivals area.

Trains & buses Run every 30 minutes from 6.30am to 11.40pm.

Night buses Hourly departures from 12.30am to 5am.

Taxis Set fare €48; 45 minutes.

Malpensa Airport (Milan)

Rental cars In Terminal 1 agencies are on the 1st floor; in Terminal 2 in the Arrivals hall.

Malpensa Express & Shuttle Runs every 30 minutes from 5am to 11pm.

Night buses Limited services from 12.15am to 5am.

Taxis Set fare €90; 50 minutes.

Capodichino Airport (Naples)

Rental cars Agencies are located in the main Arrivals hall.

Airport shuttles Run every 20 minutes from 6.30am to 11.40pm.

Taxis Set fare €19 to €23; 30 minutes.

Mobile Phones (Cell Phones)

Local SIM cards can be used in European, Australian and unlocked, multiband US phones. Other phones must be set to roaming.

Internet Access

Wi-fi is available in many lodgings and city bars, often free. Internet cafes are thin on the ground and typically charge €2 to €6 per hour.

Money

ATMs at airports, most train stations and in towns and cities. Credit cards accepted in most hotels and restaurants. Keep cash for immediate expenses.

Tipping

Not obligatory but round up the bill in pizzerias and trattorias; 10% is normal in upmarket restaurants.

Useful Websites

Italia (www.italia.it) Official tourism site.

Michelin (www.viamichelin.it) A useful route planner.

Agriturismi (www.agriturismi. it) Guide to farmstays.

Lonely Planet (www. lonelyplanet.com/italy) Destination low-down.

For more, see Road Trip Essentials (p115).

Road Trips

1 **World Heritage Wonders,** 14 days
The Colosseum, the Leaning Tower, the Galleria degli Uffizi – this trip takes in all of Italy's greatest hits. (p19)

2 **Tuscan Landscapes, 3–4 days**
Cruise through green-gold hills dotted with cypress trees and lovely Renaissance towns. (p29)

3 **Etruscan Tuscany & Lazio,** 3–4 days
The ruins of a great civilisaton set in a dramatic natural landscape. (p37)

4 **Tuscan Wine Tour,** 4 days
Slow down to a provincial pace and enjoy stunning vineyard scenery and rustic cuisine, accompanied by a fine drop or two. (p45)

Farmhouse in the Val d'Orcia (p31)
DOUGLAS PEARSON/GETTY ©

World Heritage Wonders

1

From Rome to Venice, this tour of Unesco World Heritage Sites takes in some of Italy's greatest hits, including the Colosseum and the Leaning Tower of Pisa, and some lesser-known treasures.

TRIP HIGHLIGHTS

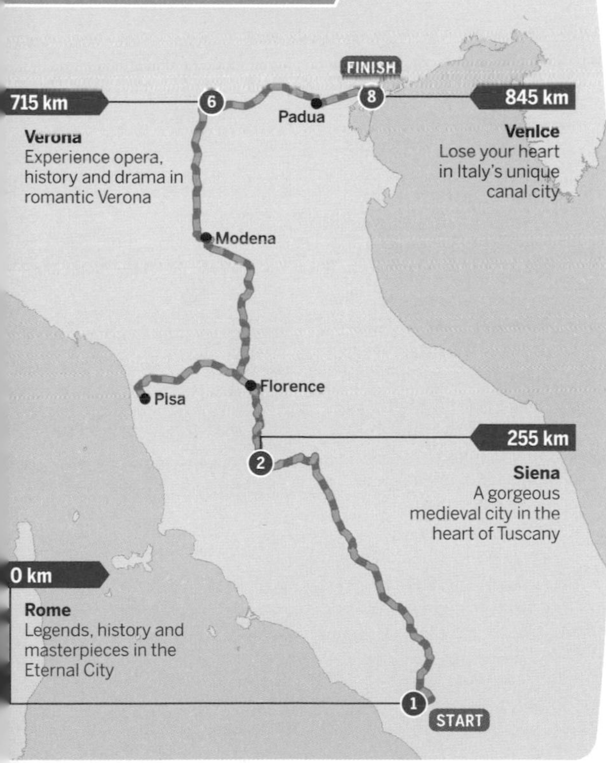

FINISH

715 km ⑥
Padua ⑧
845 km

Verona
Experience opera, history and drama in romantic Verona

● Modena

Venice
Lose your heart in Italy's unique canal city

● Pisa
● Florence

②

255 km

Siena
A gorgeous medieval city in the heart of Tuscany

0 km

Rome
Legends, history and masterpieces in the Eternal City

① **START**

14 DAYS
845KM / 525 MI

GREAT FOR...

BEST TIME TO GO
April, May and September, for ideal sightseeing weather and local produce.

ESSENTIAL PHOTO
The Roman Forum from the Palatino.

BEST FOR RENAISSANCE ART
Florence's Galleria degli Uffizi.

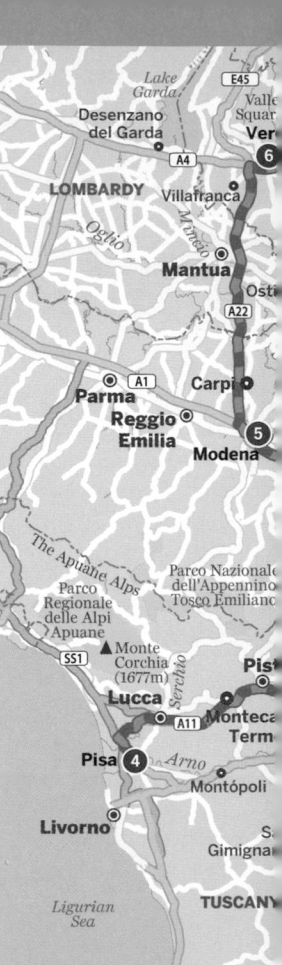

1 World Heritage Wonders

Topping the Unesco charts with 47 World Heritage Sites, Italy offers the full gamut, ranging from historic city centres and human-made masterpieces to snow-capped mountains and areas of outstanding natural beauty. This trip through central and northern Italy touches on the country's unparalleled artistic and architectural legacy, taking in ancient Roman ruins, priceless Renaissance paintings, great cathedrals and, to cap it all off, Venice's unique canal-scape.

TRIP HIGHLIGHT

❶ Rome (p98)

An epic, monumental metropolis, Italy's capital is a city of thrilling beauty and high drama. Its historic centre, which according to Unesco boasts 'some of the major monuments of antiquity', has been a World Heritage Site since 1980, and the **Vatican**, technically a separate state but in reality located within the city limits of Rome (Roma), has been on the Unesco list since 1984.

Of Rome's many ancient monuments, the most iconic is the

Colosseum (Piazza del Colosseo), the towering 1st-century-AD amphitheatre where gladiators met in mortal combat and condemned criminals fought against wild beasts. Nearby, the **Palatino** (Via di San Gregorio 30) was the ancient city's most exclusive neighbourhood, as well as its oldest – Romulus and Remus supposedly founded the city here in 753 BC. From the Palatino, you can descend to the skeletal ruins of the **Roman Forum** (Largo della Salara Vecchia), the once-beating heart of the ancient city. All three sights are covered by a single

ticket (adult/reduced
€12/7.50) and are open
from 8.30am to one hour
before sunset.

To complete your tour
of classical wonders
search out the **Pantheon**
(Piazza della Rotonda;
admission free; ⏰8.30am-
7.30pm Mon-Sat, 9am-6pm
Sun), the best preserved
of Rome's ancient
monuments. One of the
most architecturally
influential buildings in
the world, this domed
temple, now church, is an
extraordinary sight with
its martial portico and
soaring interior.

The Drive » The easiest route
to Siena, about three hours' away,
is via the A1 autostrada. Join this
from the Rome ring road, the
CRA (Grande Raccordo Anulare),
and head north, past Orvieto's
dramatic cliff-top cathedral, to
the Valdichiana exit. Take this and
follow for Siena.

LINK YOUR TRIP

3 Etruscan Tuscany & Lazio

From Rome take the A12
autostrada up to Cerveteri
and connect with this
tour of ancient Etruscan
treasures (p37).

4 Tuscan Wine Tour

From Florence head
south to Tuscany's Chianti
wine country, to indulge in
some wine tasting at the
area's historic vineyards
(p45).

❷ Siena (p74)

Siena is one of Italy's most enchanting medieval towns. Its walled centre, a beautifully preserved warren of dark lanes, Gothic *palazzi* (mansions) and pretty piazzas, is centred on **Piazza del Campo** (known as Il Campo), the sloping shell-shaped square that stages the city's annual horse race, Il Palio (p34).

On the piazza, the 102m-high **Torre del Mangia** (admission €10; ⏱10am-7pm Mar–mid-Oct, to 4pm mid-Oct–Feb) soars above the Gothic **Palazzo Comunale** (Palazzo Pubblico), home to the city's finest art museum, the **Museo Civico** (adult/reduced €9/8; ⏱10am-7pm; to 6pm winter). Of Siena's churches, the one to see is the 13th-century **Duomo** (Piazza del Duomo; summer/winter €4/free; ⏱10.30am-7pm Mon-Sat, 1.30-6pm Sun), one of Italy's greatest Gothic churches. Highlights include the remarkable white, green and red facade, and, inside, the magnificent inlaid marble floor that illustrates historical and biblical stories.

The Drive >> There are two alternatives to get to Florence. The quickest, which is via the fast RA3 Siena–Firenze Raccordo, takes about 1½ hours. But if you have the time, we recommend the scenic SR222, which snakes through the Chianti wine country, passing through quintessential hilltop towns and vine-laden slopes. Reckon on at least 2½ hours for this route.

❸ Florence (p56)

Cradle of the Renaissance and home of Michelangelo, Machiavelli and the Medici, Florence (Firenze) is magnetic, romantic, unique and busy. A couple of days is not long here, but it's enough for a breathless introduction to the city's top sights.

Towering above the medieval skyline, the imposing **Duomo** (Piazza del Duomo; admission free ⏱10am-5pm Mon-Wed & Fri, to 4.30pm Thu, to 4.45pm Sat, 1.30-4.45pm Sun) dominates the city centre with its famous red-tiled dome and striking facade. A short hop away, **Piazza della Signoria** opens onto the sculpture-filled **Loggia dei Lanzi** and the **Torre d'Arnolfo** above **Palazzo Vecchio** (www. musefirenze.it; Piazza della Signoria; adult/reduced €10/8; ⏱9am-midnight Fri-Wed, to 2pm Thu summer), Florence's lavish City Hall.

↱ DETOUR: SAN GIMIGNANO

Start: ❷ **Siena**

Dubbed the medieval Manhattan thanks to its 15 11th-century towers, San Gimignano is a classic hilltop town and an easy detour from Siena.

From the car park next to Porta San Giovanni, it's a short walk up to **Palazzo Comunale** (Piazza del Duomo; admission €5; ⏱9.30am-7pm Apr-Sep, 10am-5.30pm Oct-Mar), which houses the town's art gallery, the **Pinacoteca**, and tallest tower, the **Torre Grossa**. Nearby, the Romanesque basilica, known as the **Collegiata** (Piazza del Duomo; adult/child €3.50/1.50; ⏱10am-7.10pm Mon-Fri, to 5.10pm Sat, 12.30-7.10pm Sun, closed 2nd half of Nov & Jan), boasts some remarkable Ghirlandaio frescoes.

Before leaving town, be sure to sample the local Vernaccia wine at the **Museo del Vino** (Wine Museum; Parco della Rocca; admission free, tastings 4/6 wines €6/10; ⏱11.30am-6.30pm) next to the Rocca (fortress).

San Gimignano is about 40km northwest of Siena. Head for Florence until Poggibonsi and then pick up the SS429.

Next to the *palazzo*, the **Galleria degli Uffizi** (Uffizi Gallery; www.uffizi. firenze.it; Piazza degli Uffizi 6; adult/reduced €8/4, plus exhibition supplement; ⊙8.15am-6.50pm Tue-Sun) houses one of the world's great art collections, including works by Botticelli, Leonardo da Vinci, Michelangelo, Raphael and many other Renaissance maestros. For a walk through the heart of Florence, flip to our walking tour (p62).

The Drive » From Florence it's about 1½ hours to Pisa along the A11 autostrada. At the end of the motorway, after the toll booth, head left onto Via Aurelia (SS1) and follow signs to Pisa Centro.

- - - - - - - - - - - -

❹ Pisa (p88)

Once a maritime republic to rival Genoa and Venice, Pisa now owes its fame to an architectural project gone horribly wrong. The **Leaning Tower of Pisa** (Torre Pendente) is an extraordinary sight and one of Italy's most photographed monuments. The tower, originally erected as a *campanile* (bell tower) from the late 12th century, is one of three Romanesque buildings on the immaculate lawns of **Piazza dei Miracoli** (also known as Campo dei Miracoli or Piazza del Duomo).

The candy-striped **Duomo** (admission free

WORLD HERITAGE SITES

With 47 World Heritage Sites, Italy has more than any other country. But what exactly is a World Heritage Site? Basically it's anywhere that Unesco's World Heritage Committee decides is of 'outstanding universal value' and inscribes on the World Heritage List. It could be a natural wonder such as the Great Barrier Reef in Australia or a constructed icon such as New York's Statue of Liberty, a historic city centre or a great work of art or architecture.

The list was set up in 1972 and has since grown to include 962 sites from 157 countries. Italy first got in on the act in 1979 when it successfully nominated its first entry – the prehistoric rock drawings of the Valcamonica valley in northeastern Lombardy. The inscription process requires sites to be nominated by a country and then independently evaluated. If they pass scrutiny and meet at least one of 10 selection criteria, they get the green light at the World Heritage Committee's annual meeting. Once on the list, sites qualify for management support and access to the World Heritage Fund.

Italian nominations have generally fared well and since Rome's historic centre and the Chiesa di Santa Maria delle Grazie in Milan were inscribed in 1980, many of the nation's greatest attractions have made it on to the list – the historic centres of Florence, Naples, Siena and San Gimignano; the cities of Venice, Verona and Ferrara; the archaeological sites of Pompeii, Paestum and Agrigento; as well as natural beauties such as the Amalfi Coast, Aeolian Islands, Dolomites and Tuscany's Val d'Orcia.

⊙10am-8pm summer, 10am-12.45pm & 2-5pm winter), begun in 1063, has a graceful tiered facade and cavernous interior, while to its west, the cupcake-like **Battistero** (Baptistery; adult/reduced €5/3 ⊙8am-8pm summer, 10am-5pm Nov-Feb) is something of an architectural hybrid, with a Pisan-Romanesque lower section and a Gothic upper level and dome.

The Drive » It's a 2½-hour drive up to Modena from Pisa. Head back towards Florence on the A11 and then pick up the A1 to Bologna. Continue as the road twists and falls through the wooded Apennines before flattening out near Bologna. Exit at Modena Sud (Modena South) and follow for the Centro.

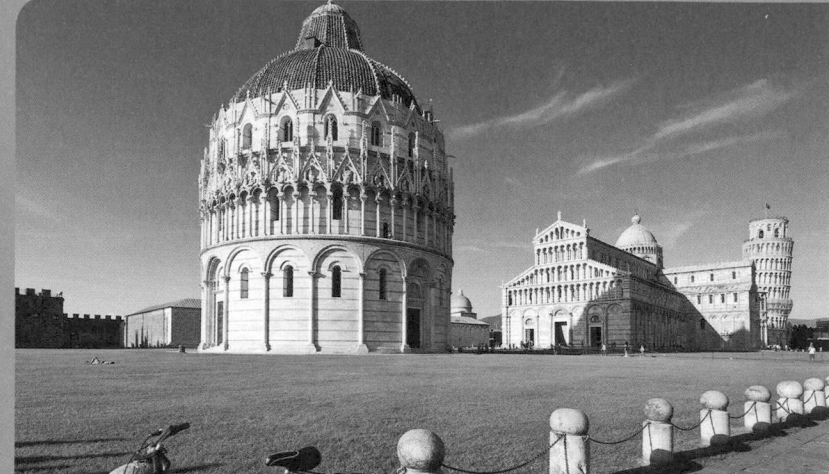

WHY THIS IS A CLASSIC TRIP
DUNCAN GARWOOD, AUTHOR

Every one of the towns and cities on this drive is special. The great treasures of Rome, Florence and Venice are amazing but, for me, it's the lesser-known highlights that make this such an incredible trip – Modena's stunning Romanesque cathedral, the Scrovegni Chapel in Padua, and Verona's gorgeous medieval centre.

Top: Pisa's Piazza dei Miracoli (p23)
Left: *Tigelle*, a traditional street food of Modena
Right: The towers of San Gimignano (p22)

MATTES REN/HEMIS.FR/GETTY IMAGES ©

GABBIERE/GETTY IMAGES ©

⑤ Modena

One of Italy's top foodie towns, Modena boasts a stunning medieval centre and a trio of Unesco-listed sights. First up is the gorgeous **cathedral** (Corso Duomo; ☺7am-12.30pm & 3.30-7pm), which is widely considered to be Italy's finest Romanesque church. Features to look out for include the Gothic rose window and a series of bas-reliefs depicting scenes from Genesis.

Nearby, the 13th-century **Torre Ghirlandina** (Piazza Torre; admission €3; 9.30am-1pm & 3-7pm Tue-Fri, 9.30am-7pm Sat & Sun Apr-Sep, to 5.30pm Oct-Mar), an 87m-high tower topped by a Gothic spire, was named after Seville's Giralda bell tower by exiled Spanish Jews in the early 16th century. The last of the Unesco threesome is **Piazza Grande**, just south of the cathedral. The city's focal square, this is flanked by the porticoed Palazzo Comunale, Modena's elegant town hall.

The Drive » From Modena reckon on about 1¼ hours to Verona, via the A1 and A22 autostradas. Follow the A22 as it traverses the flat Po valley plain, passing the medieval town of Mantua (Mantova; worth a quick break) before connecting with the A4. Turn off at Verona Sud and follow signs for the Centro.

ITALIAN ART & ARCHITECTURE

The Ancients

In pre-Roman times, the Greeks built theatres and proportionally perfect temples in their southern colonies at Agrigento, Syracuse and Paestum, whilst the Etruscans concentrated on funerary art, creating elaborate tombs at Tarquinia and Cerveteri. Coming in their wake, the Romans specialised in roads, aqueducts and monumental amphitheatres such as the Colosseum and Verona's Arena.

Romanesque

With the advent of Christianity in the 4th century, basilicas began to spring up, many with glittering Byzantine-style mosaics. The Romanesque period (c 1050–1200) saw the construction of fortified monasteries and robust, bulky churches such as Bari's Basilica di San Nicola and Modena's cathedral. Pisa's striking *duomo* (cathedral) displays a characteristic Tuscan variation on the style.

Gothic

Gothic architecture, epic in scale and typically embellished by gargoyles, pinnacles and statues, took on a more classical form in Italy. Assisi's Basilica di San Francesco is an outstanding early example, but for the full-blown Italian Gothic style check out the cathedrals in Florence, Venice, Siena and Orvieto.

Renaissance

From quiet beginnings in 14th-century Florence, the Renaissance erupted across Italy before spreading across Europe. In Italy, painters such as Giotto, Botticelli, Leonardo da Vinci and Raphael led the way, while architects Brunelleschi and Bramante rewrote the rule books with their beautifully proportioned basilicas. All-rounder Michelangelo worked his way into immortality, producing masterpieces such as *David* and the Sistine Chapel frescoes.

Baroque

Dominating the 17th century, the extravagant baroque style found fertile soil in Italy. Witness the Roman works of Gian Lorenzo Bernini and Francesco Borromini, Lecce's flamboyant *centro storico* (historic centre) and the magical baroque towns of southeastern Sicily.

Neoclassicism

Signalling a return to sober classical lines, neoclassicism ruled in the late 18th and early 19th centuries. Signature works include Caserta's Palazzo Reale and La Scala opera house in Milan. In artistic terms, the most famous Italian exponent was Antonio Canova.

TRIP HIGHLIGHT

❻ Verona

A World Heritage Site since 2000, Verona's historic centre is a beautiful compilation of architectural styles and inspiring buildings. Chief among these is its stunning Roman amphitheatre, known as the **Arena** (☎045 800 51 51; www.arena.it; Piazza Brà; adult/student/child €4/3/1; ⊙tours 1.45-7.30pm Mon & 8.30am-7.30pm Tue-Sun Oct-May, 8am-3.30pm Jun-Aug). Dating to the 1st century AD, this is Italy's third-largest amphitheatre after the Colosseum and Capua amphitheatre, and although it can no longer seat 30,000, it still draws sizeable crowds to its opera and music concerts.

From the Arena, it's an easy walk to the river Adige and **Castelvecchio** (Corso Castelvecchio 2; adult/reduced €6/4.50; ◷1.30-7.30pm Mon, 8.30am-7.30pm Tue-Sun), Verona's picturesque castle and top art museum. Like many of the city's outstanding monuments, this was built during the 14th-century reign of the tyrannical Della Scala (Scaligeri) family, whose eye-catching Gothic tombs, the **Arche Scaligere** (Via Arche Scaligere), stand near elegant Piazza dei Signori.

The Drive » To Padua it's about an hour from Verona on the A4 Venice autostrada. Exit at Padova Ovest (Padua West) and join the SP47 after the toll booth. Follow this until you see, after a road bridge, a turn-off signposted to the Centro.

- - - - - - - - - - - - - - -

❼ Padua

Travellers to Padua (Padova) usually make a beeline for the city's main attraction, the **Scrovegni Chapel** (☎049 201 00 20; www.cappelladegliscrovegni. it; Giardini dell'Arena; adult/reduced €13/8; ◷9am-7pm by reservation), but there's more to Padua

than Giotto frescoes and it's actually the **Orto Botanico** (www. ortobotanicopd.it; adult/reduced €10/8; 9am-7pm Tue-Sun, to 6pm Oct, to 5pm Nov-Mar) that represents Padua on Unesco's list of World Heritage Sites. The oldest botanical garden in the world, this dates to 1545 when a group of medical students planted some rare plants in order to study their medicinal properties. A short walk from the garden, Padua's vast **Basilica di Sant'Antonio** (www. basilicadelsanto.org; Piazza del Santo; ◷6.20am-7.45pm Apr-Oct, to 6.45pm Nov-Mar) is a major pilgrimage destination, attracting thousands of visitors a year who pay homage to St Anthony, the city's patron saint, who is buried here.

The Drive » Traffic permitting, it's about 45 minutes from Padua to Venice, along the A4. Pass through industrial Mestre and over the Ponte della Libertà lagoon bridge to the car park on Piazzale Roma.

- - - - - - - - - - - - - - -

TRIP HIGHLIGHT

❽ Venice

The end of the road, quite literally, is Venice (Venezia). Of the city's many must-sees the most famous are on Piazza

San Marco, including the **Basilica di San Marco** (www.basilicasanmarco. it; Piazza San Marco; ◷9.45am-5pm Mon-Sat, 2-4pm Sun), Venice's great showpiece church. Built originally to house the bones of St Mark, it's a truly awe-inspiring vision with its spangled spires, Byzantine domes, luminous mosaics and lavish marble work. For a bird's-eye view, head to the nearby **campanile** (bell tower; admission €8; ◷9am-9pm summer, to 7pm spring & autumn, 9.30am-3.45pm winter).

Adjacent to the basilica, the **Palazzo Ducale** (Piazzetta San Marco; adult/reduced €18/11; ◷8.30am-7pm summer, to 5.30pm winter) was the official residence of Venice's doges (ruling dukes) from the 9th century. Inside, its lavishly decorated chambers harbour some seriously heavyweight art, including Tintoretto's gigantic *Paradiso* (Paradise) in the Sala del Maggior Consiglio. Connecting the palace to the city dungeons, the **Ponte dei Sospiri** (Bridge of Sighs) was named after the sighs that prisoners – including Casanova – emitted en route from court to cell.

Tuscan Landscapes

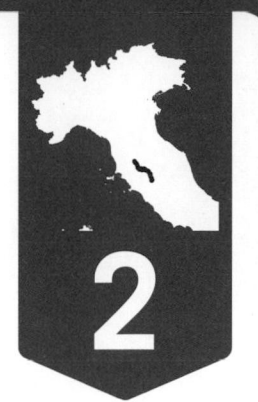

2

Rolling hills capped by medieval towns, golden wheat fields and snaking lines of cypress trees – immerse yourself in Tuscan scenery on this trip through the region's southern stretches.

TRIP HIGHLIGHTS

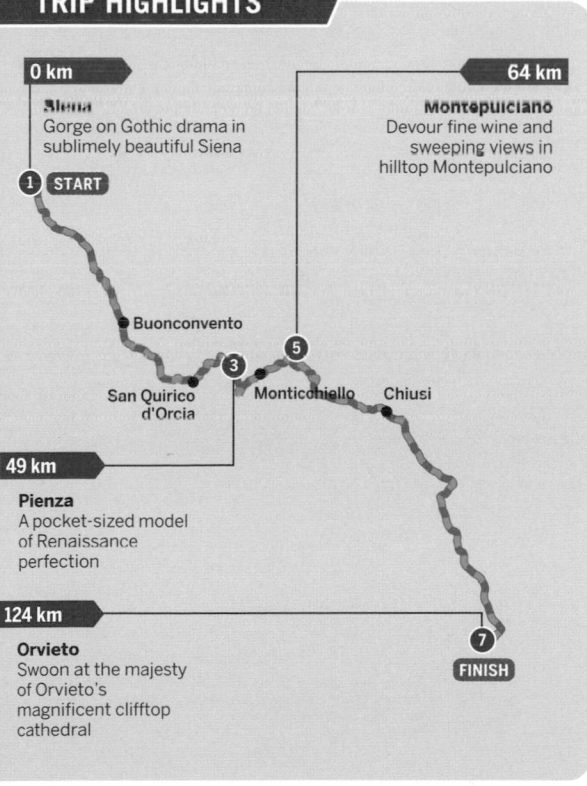

0 km

Siena
Gorge on Gothic drama in sublimely beautiful Siena

64 km

Montepulciano
Devour fine wine and sweeping views in hilltop Montepulciano

1 START
Buonconvento
3
San Quirico d'Orcia
5
Monticchiello
Chiusi
7
FINISH

49 km

Pienza
A pocket-sized model of Renaissance perfection

124 km

Orvieto
Swoon at the majesty of Orvieto's magnificent clifftop cathedral

3–4 DAYS
124KM / 77 MILES

GREAT FOR...

BEST TIME TO GO
May to September for blue skies and fab photos.

ESSENTIAL PHOTO
The Val d'Orcia between San Quirico d'Orcia and Pienza.

BEST FOR RENAISSANCE ARCHITECTURE
Montepulciano's historic centre.

eft Villa in a valley near Pienza (p32)

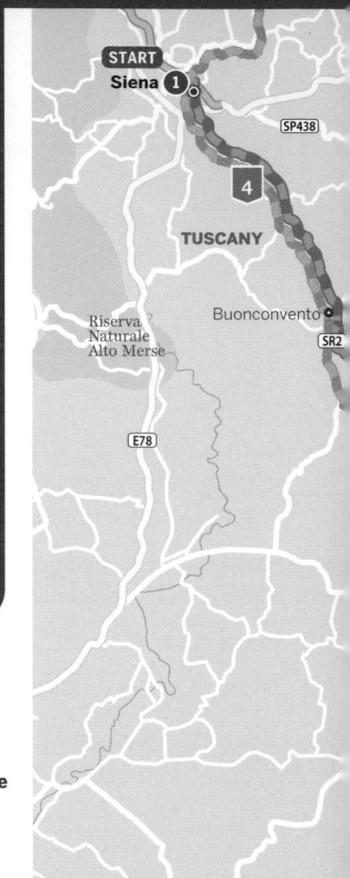

2 Tuscan Landscapes

Ever since medieval pilgrims discovered Tuscany en route from Canterbury to Rome, the region has been captivating travellers. This trip strikes south from Siena, running through the Crete Senesi – an area of clay hills scored by deep ravines – to the Unesco-listed Val d'Orcia, whose soothing hills and billowing plains are punctuated by delightful Renaissance towns. The end of the road is Orvieto, home to one of Italy's most feted Gothic cathedrals.

TRIP HIGHLIGHT

❶ Siena (p74)

With its medieval *palazzi* (mansions) and humbling Gothic architecture, Siena's historic centre is a sight to compare with any in Tuscany. To admire it from above, climb to the top of the **Torre del Mangia** (admission €10; ⏰10am-7pm Mar–mid-Oct, to 4pm mid-Oct–Feb), the slender 14th-century tower that rises above **Piazza del Campo**, and look down on a sea of red-tiled roofs and, beyond, to the green, undulating countryside that awaits you on this trip.

At the foot of the tower, **Palazzo Comunale** (Palazzo Pubblico) is a magnificent example of Sienese Gothic architecture and home to the city's best art museum, the **Museo Civico** (adult/reduced €9/8; ⏰10am-7pm; to 6pm winter).

To the southwest of Palazzo Pubblico, another inspiring spectacle awaits. Siena's 13th-century **Duomo** (Piazza del Duomo; summer/winter €4/free; ⏰10.30am-7pm Mon-Sat, 1.30-6pm Sun) is one of Italy's greatest Gothic churches, and its magnificent facade of white, green and red polychrome marble is one you'll remember long after you've left town.

The Drive » The first leg down to San Quirico d'Orcia, about an hour's drive, takes you down the scenic SR2 via the market town of Buonconvento. En route you'll pass cultivated fields and swaths of curvaceous green plains.

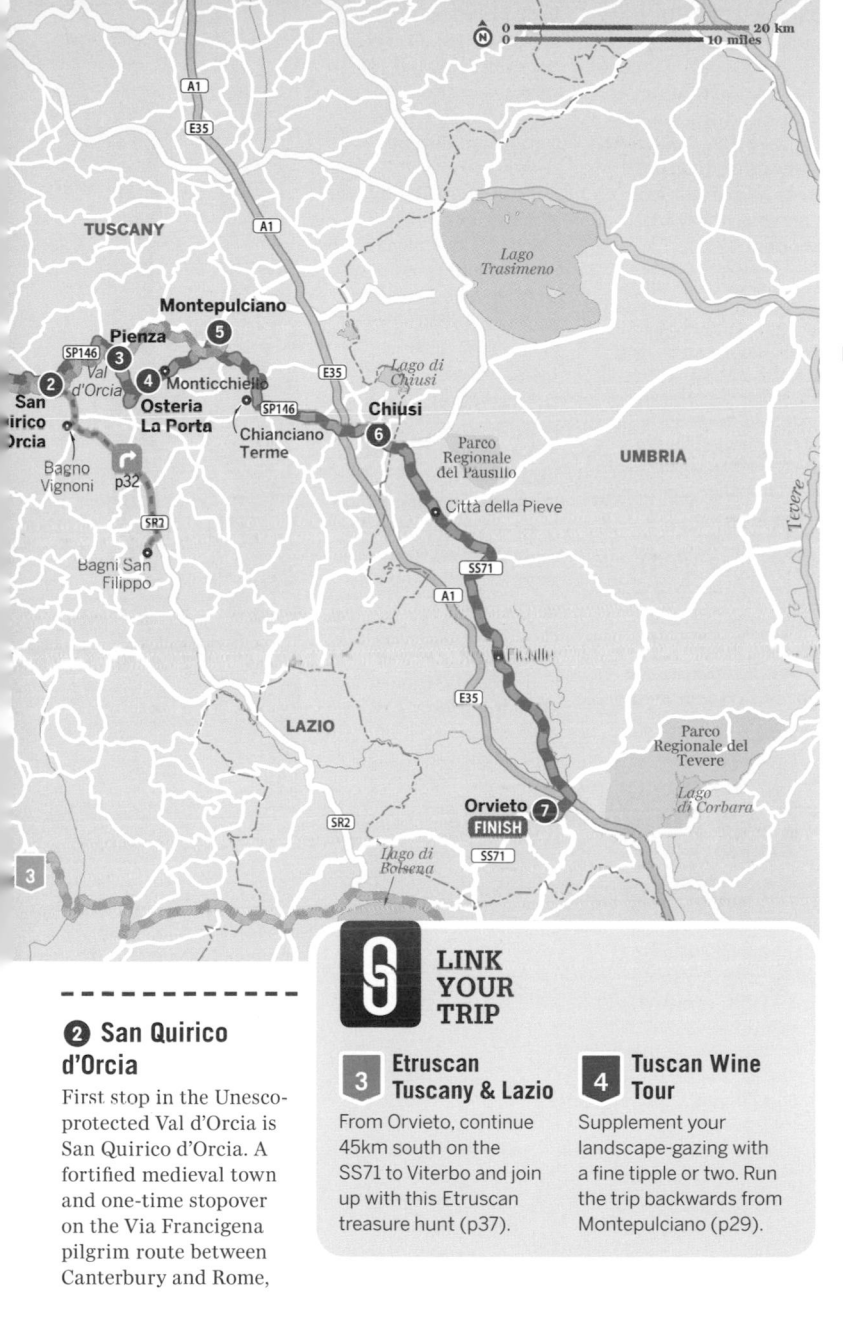

TUSCANY 2 TUSCAN LANDSCAPES

❷ San Quirico d'Orcia

First stop in the Unesco-protected Val d'Orcia is San Quirico d'Orcia. A fortified medieval town and one-time stopover on the Via Francigena pilgrim route between Canterbury and Rome,

![LINK YOUR TRIP logo]

LINK YOUR TRIP

3 **Etruscan Tuscany & Lazio**

From Orvieto, continue 45km south on the SS71 to Viterbo and join up with this Etruscan treasure hunt (p37).

4 **Tuscan Wine Tour**

Supplement your landscape-gazing with a fine tipple or two. Run the trip backwards from Montepulciano (p29).

it's now a lovely, low-key village. There are no great must-see sights but it's a pleasant place for a stroll, with a graceful Romanesque **Collegiata** (church) and formal Renaissance gardens known as the **Horti Leononi**.

The Drive » From San Quirico d'Orcia it's a quick 15-minute drive to Pienza along the SP146. This is one of the trip's most beautiful stretches, offering unfettered views over seas of undulating grasslands peppered by stone farmhouses and lines of elegant cypress trees.

TRIP HIGHLIGHT

❸ Pienza (p84)

One of the most popular hill towns in the Val d'Orcia, pint-sized Pienza boasts a Renaissance centre that has changed

HIROSHI HIGUCHI/GETTY IMAGES ©

little since local boy Pope Pius II had it built between 1459 and 1462. Action is centred on Piazza Pio II, where the solemn **duomo** (🕐8.30am-1pm & 2.15-6.30pm) is flanked by two Renaissance *palazzi* – on the right, **Palazzo Piccolomini** (www.palazzopiccolominipienza.it; guided tours adult/reduced €7/5; 🕐10am-6.30pm Tue-Sun mid-Mar–mid-Oct, to 4.30pm mid-Oct–mid-Mar), the former papal residence; on the left, Palazzo Vescovile, home to the **Museo Diocesano** (Corso Rossellino 30; adult/reduced €4.50/3; 🕐10am-1pm & 2-5pm Wed-Mon summer, 10am-4pm Sat & Sun winter) and an intriguing miscellany of artworks, manuscripts, tapestries and miniatures. Before leaving town make sure you pick up some local *pecorino* cheese for which the area is justly famous.

The Drive » From Pienza strike south on the SP18 and head into the heart of the countryside, enjoying more bucolic scenery as you go. After 6km or so you'll see a sign to Monticchiello off to the left. Take this and continue for another 4km.

DETOUR: BAGNO VIGNONI & BAGNI SAN FILIPPO

Start: ❷ San Quirico d'Orcia

Some 5km south of San Quirico d'Orcia along the SR2, hot sulphurous water (around 49°C) bubbles up into a picturesque pool in the centre of **Bagno Vignoni**. You can't actually enter the pool but there are various spa complexes offering a full range of treatments. For free hot-water frolics continue 15km further along the SR2 to the tiny village of **Bagni San Filippo**, where there are thermal cascades in an open-air reserve. You'll find these just uphill from Hotel le Terme – follow a sign marked 'Fosso Bianco' down a lane for about 150m to limestone outcrops, and you'll come to a set of warm, tumbling cascades that get more spectacular the further downhill you walk. It's a pleasant if slightly whiffy spot for a picnic.

Pienza

❹ Osteria La Porta

A 15-minute drive
southeast from
Pienza brings you to
Monticchiello, a sleepy
medieval hilltop village.
Just inside the main
gate, the highly regarded
Osteria La Porta (☎0578
75 51 63; Via del Piano 3; meals
€40; ⊘Fri-Wed) has a small
terrace with panoramic
views of the Val d'Orcia
and a reputation for

food and service that
behoves a reservation,
even in low season. The
fixed menu at lunchtime
offers great value, and
spuntini (snacks) such
as bruschetta, olives and
cheese plates are served
outside usual meal hours.

The Drive » Take the SP88
and follow it as it ploughs
on through fields and light
woodland to the main SP146. Go
left and continue past orderly
vineyards and olive groves up

to San Biagio and 2km further
on to Montepulciano. All told it's
about 20 minutes.

TRIP HIGHLIGHT

❺ Montepulciano (p85)

Famous for its
Vino Nobile wine,
Montepulciano is a
steeply stacked hill
town harbouring a
wealth of *palazzi* and
fine buildings, as well as

grandstand views over the Val di Chiana and Val d'Orcia. The main street, aka **Il Corso**, climbs steeply, passing **Caffè Poliziano**, which has been operating since 1868, as it leads to the **Cantine Contucci** (www.contucci.it; Via del Teatro 1; admission free, fee for tastings; ⊙9.30am-12.30pm & 2.30-6pm), one of two historic wine cellars in town. Nearby **Piazza Grande** is flanked by the 14th-century **Palazzo Comunale** (access to panoramic terrace/tower €3;/5 ⊙10am-6pm Mon-Sat) and late-16th-century **duomo** (⊙8am-6pm).

The Drive » Reckon on about 40 minutes to cover the 25km to Chiusi. From Montepulciano head southeast along the SP146 to Chianciano Terme, a popular spa town. Continue on towards the A1 autostrada, and Chiusi is just on the other side of the highway.

6 Chiusi

Once an important Etruscan centre, Chiusi is now a sleepy country town. Its main attractions are the Etruscan tombs dotted around the surrounding countryside, two of which are included in the ticket price of the **Museo Archeologico Nazionale** (☎0578 20 1 77; Via Porsenna 93; adult/reduced €6/3; ⊙9am-8pm). In town, you can go underground in the **Labirinto di Porsenna** (Museo della Cattedrale, Piazza Duomo; admission €3; ⊙10am-12.45pm & 4-6.30pm Jun-Oct, shorter hrs rest of yr), a series of tunnels dating to Etruscan times that formed part of the town's water supply system.

The Drive » You have two choices for Orvieto. The quick route is on the A1 autostrada (about 45 minutes), but it's a more interesting drive along the SS71 (1½ hours). This passes through Città della Pieve, birthplace of the painter Perugino, and Ficulle, known since Roman times for its artisans.

TRIP HIGHLIGHT

7 Orvieto

Over the regional border in Umbria, the precariously perched town of Orvieto boasts one of Italy's finest Gothic cathedrals. The **Cattedrale di Orvieto** (www.opsm.it; Piazza Duomo; admission €2, incl Cappella di San Brizio €3; ⊙9.30am-6pm Apr-Oct, 9.30am-1pm & 2.30-5pm Nov-Mar) took 30 years to plan and three centuries to complete. Work began in 1290, originally to a Romanesque design, but as construction proceeded, Gothic features were incorporated into the structure. Highlights include the richly coloured facade, and, in the **Cappella di San Brizio**, Luca Signorelli's fresco cycle *The Last Judgement*.

Across the piazza from the cathedral, the **Museo Claudio Faina e Civico** (www.museofaina.it; Piazza Duomo 29; adult/reduced €4.50/3; ⊙9.30am-6pm Apr-Sep, 10am-5pm Tue-Sun Oct-Mar) houses an important collection of Etruscan archaeological artefacts.

THE PALIO

Siena's Palio is one of Italy's most spectacular annual events. Dating from the Middle Ages, it comprises a series of colourful pageants and a wild horse race on 2 July and 16 August. Ten of Siena's 17 *contrade* (town districts) compete for the coveted *palio* (silk banner).

From about 5pm, representatives from each *contrada* parade around the Campo in historical costume, all bearing their individual banners. Then, at 7.45pm in July and 7pm in August, the race gets the green light. For scarcely one exhilarating minute, the 10 horses and their bareback riders tear three times around the temporarily constructed dirt racetrack with a speed and violence that makes spectators' hair stand on end.

Etruscan Tuscany & Lazio

3

From Tuscan seascapes and rugged hilltop towns to tufa-carved tombs and raunchy frescoes, this tour takes you into the heart of ancient Etruria, the land the Etruscans once called home.

TRIP HIGHLIGHTS

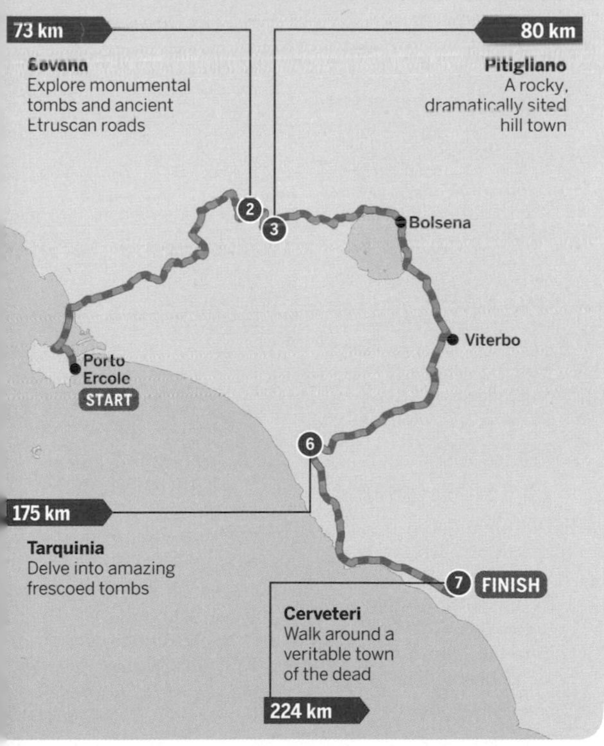

73 km

Sovana
Explore monumental tombs and ancient Etruscan roads

80 km

Pitigliano
A rocky, dramatically sited hill town

● Bolsena

② ③

● Viterbo

Porto Ercole
START

⑥

175 km

Tarquinia
Delve into amazing frescoed tombs

⑦ FINISH

Cerveteri
Walk around a veritable town of the dead

224 km

3–4 DAYS
224KM / 139 MILES

GREAT FOR...

BEST TIME TO GO
Early summer is good for sightseeing and the sea.

ESSENTIAL PHOTO
Pitigliano rising out of the rock.

BEST FOR HIKING
Etruscan trails around Sovana and Pitigliano.

t Rocca Monaldeschi fortress (p40)

3 Etruscan Tuscany & Lazio

Long before Rome came into existence, the Etruscans had forged a great civilisation in the pitted, rugged hills of southern Tuscany, Umbria and northern Lazio. This trip leads through these little-known parts of the country, opening the window onto dramatic natural scenery and spectacular Etruscan treasures. From Tuscany's pock-marked peaks to the haunting tombs that litter Lazio's soft green slopes, it's a beguiling ride.

❶ Porto Ercole, Monte Argentario

To warm you up for the road ahead, spend some time exploring Monte Argentario, a rugged promontory just off the southern Tuscan coast. The more appealing of its two towns is Porto Ercole, an attractive harbour nestled between three Spanish forts on the promontory's less-crowded eastern side. This is where Caravaggio died in 1610, and although it's fairly short on traditional attractions its hillside *centro storico* (historic centre) is a charming place for a stroll. Continue to the top, past the **Chiesa di Sant'Erasmo** (Piazza Santa Barbara) to the **Rocca fort** and you're rewarded with magnificent views.

The Drive >> Reckon on about 1¾ hours for this first leg. Cross the water over to Albinia and join the eastbound SS74. Follow this through expanses of farmland up to Manciano, before turning left onto the SS322. Continue through Montemerano and the Terme di Saturnia before curving back to Sovana.

TRIP HIGHLIGHT

❷ Sovana (p87)

Tuscany's most significant Etruscan tombs are concentrated in the **Parco Archeologico della Città del Tufa** (www.leviecave.it), an archaeological park encompassing land around the villages of Sovana, Sorano and Vitozza. At Sovana, the best finds are in the **Necropolis** (admission €5; ⊙10am-7pm summer, shorter hrs winter), just 1.5km west of the village. Here you'll find four major tombs, including the monumental **Tomba Ildebranda**, with traces of carved columns and stairs, as well as two stretches of original Etruscan road – **Via del Cavone** and **Via Cava di Poggio Prisca**.

The village itself boasts a pretty main street and two beautiful Romanesque churches – the **Duomo** (🕙10am-1pm & 2.30-6pm summer, shorter hrs winter), with its austere vaulted interior, and the **Chiesa di Santa Maria Maggiore** (🕙daily summer, Sat & Sun rest of yr), notable for its 16th-century apse frescoes.

The Drive » Head east out of Sovana and after a couple of kilometres go right on the SP46. This winding road twists through scorched open peaks and

LINK YOUR TRIP

2 Tuscan Landscapes

From Bolsena, take the SS2 Via Cassia 65km north to San Quirico d'Orcia, one of the gems in Tuscany's stunning Val d'Orcia (p29).

occasional pockets of woodland as it descends to Pitigliano, about 10 minutes away.

---

❸ Pitigliano (p87)

Sprouting from a towering tufa outcrop and surrounded by dramatic gorges on three sides, Pitigliano is a lovely knot of twisting stairways, cobbled alleys and quaint stone houses. In the middle of it all, the **Museo Civico Archeologico della Civiltà Etrusca** (Piazza della Fortezza; adult/child €3/2; ⊙10am-5pm Thu-Mon) has a small but rich collection of local Etruscan finds, including some huge *bucchero* (black earthenware pottery) dating from the 6th century BC.

The town also has an interesting Jewish history – at one point it was dubbed 'Little Jerusalem' – which you can find out about at **La Piccola Gerusalemme** (www.lapiccolagerusalemme. it; Vicolo Manin 30; adult/ reduced €4/3; ⊙10am-1pm & 2.30-6pm Sun-Fri Apr-Sep, 10am-noon & 3-5pm Sun-Fri Oct-Mar).

The Drive » Head east on the SS74 until the road forks. Bear right for Gradoli and follow through the increasingly lush countryside until you hit the fast-flowing SS2 (Via Cassia). Go right and skirt the lake's northern banks into Bolsena. All told it should take about half an hour.

❹ Bolsena

The main town on **Lago di Bolsena**, Italy's largest volcanic lake, Bolsena was a major medieval pilgrimage destination after a miracle supposedly took place here in 1263, leading Pope Urban IV to establish the festival of Corpus Domini. Other than the lake, the main reason to stop by is to visit the **Rocca Monaldeschi**, a 13th-century fortress that dominates the skyline and houses a small collection of locally unearthed artefacts in the **Museo Territoriale del Lago di Bolsena** (Piazza Monaldeschi 1; adult/ reduced €5/3.50; ⊙10am-1pm & 4-9pm Tue-Sun Jun-Sep, shorter hrs rest of yr).

The Drive » It's a straightforward 50-minute drive to Viterbo along the SS2. This takes you down Lago di Bolsena's eastern side, past orchards, vineyards and olive groves through the medieval town of Montefiascone and on to Viterbo.

---

❺ Viterbo (p112)

Founded by the Etruscans and eventually taken over by Rome (Roma), Viterbo was an important medieval centre, and in the 13th century became the residence of the popes. Its Etruscan past is chronicled at the **Museo Nazionale Etrusco**

(Piazza della Rocca; adult/ reduced €6/€3; ⊙8.30am-7.30pm Tue-Sun), one of several interesting sights in the walled *centro storico*. To the south, the Renaissance **Piazza del Plebiscito** is overlooked by **Palazzo dei Priori** (Piazza del Plebiscito; admission free; ⊙9am-1pm & 3-6.30pm), Viterbo's city hall, which boasts some fine

Pitigliano

16th-century frescoes. Southwest of here, **Piazza San Lorenzo** was the medieval city's religious heart, where cardinals came to vote for their popes and pray in the 12th-century **Cattedrale di San Lorenzo**.

Next door, the **Museo del Colle del Duomo** (adult/incl guided visit to Palazzo dei Papi, Sala del Conclave & Loggia €3/9; ⏰10am-1pm & 3-7pm Tue-Sun, to 6pm winter) displays a small collection of religious artefacts, including a reliquary said to contain the chin (!) of John the Baptist. The adjacent **Palazzo dei Papi** was built in the 13th century to entice the papacy away from Rome. Its main feature is the **Sala del Conclave**, an impressive hall where five popes were elected.

The Drive › Exit Viterbo and pick up the SS675 heading towards Rome. Continue on this fast dual carriageway until the turn-off for SS2 (Via Cassia). Take this and continue to Vetralla, where you should go right onto the SS1bis (Via Aurelia bis) and continue on to Tarquinia. Allow 50 minutes all told.

THE ETRUSCANS

Of the many Italic tribes that emerged from the Stone Age, the Etruscans left the most enduring mark. By the 7th century BC their city-states – places such as Caere (modern-day Cerveteri), Tarquinii (Tarquinia), Veii (Veio), Perusia (Perugia), Volaterrae (Volterra) and Arretium (Arezzo) – were the dominant forces in central Italy.

Debate rages about their origins – Roman historian Herodotus claimed they came to Italy from Asia Minor to escape famine – but what is not disputed is that they gave rise to a sophisticated society based on agriculture, trade and mineral mining. They were skilled architects, and although little remains of their buildings, archaeologists have found evidence of aqueducts, bridges and sewers, as well as temples. In artistic terms, they were known for their jewellery and tomb decoration, producing elaborate stone sarcophagi and bright, vivid frescoes.

For much of their existence, they were rivals of the Greeks, who had colonised large tracts of southern Italy from the 8th century BC, but in the end it was the Romans who finally conquered them. In 396 BC they lost the key town of Veii, and by the 2nd century BC they and their land had largely been incorporated into the rapidly expanding Roman Republic.

TRIP HIGHLIGHT

➏ Tarquinia (p111)

The pick of Lazio's Etruscan towns, Tarquinia is a gem. Its highlight is the 7th-century-BC **Necropoli di Monterozzi** (Via Ripagretta; adult/child €6/3, incl museum €8/4; ☺8.30am-1hr before sunset Tue-Sun), one of Italy's most important Etruscan sites. Some 6000 tombs have been excavated here since 1489, of which 20 are open to the public, including the **Tomba della Caccia e della Pesca**, the richly decorated **Tomba dei Leopardi**, and the **Tomba della Fustigazione** with its erotic depiction of ancient S&M.

In the *centro storico,* the **Museo Archeologico Nazionale Tarquiniense** (Piazza Cavour; adult/child €6/3, incl Necropolis €8/4; ☺8.30am-7.30pm Tue-Sun) is a delightful museum, showcasing some wonderful Etruscan artefacts, including a breathtaking terracotta frieze of winged horses (the Cavalli Alati).

The Drive » The easiest way to Cerveteri, about 45 minutes away, is by the A12 autostrada. Take this towards Roma/Civitavecchia and exit at the Cerveteri/Ladispoli turn-off. After the toll booth, head left into town.

- - - - - - - - - - - -

TRIP HIGHLIGHT

➐ Cerveteri (p110)

Cerveteri, or Kysry to the Etruscans and Caere to Latin-speakers, was one of the most important commercial centres in the Mediterranean from the 7th to the 5th century BC.

The main sight is the Unesco-listed **Necropoli di Banditaccia** (Via del Necropoli; adult/reduced €8/5, incl museum €10/6; ☺8.30am-1hr before sunset) just outside town. This 10-hectare site is laid out like a town of the dead, with streets, squares and terraces of *tumuli* (circular tomb structures cut into the earth and capped with turf). Some of the major tombs, including the 6th-century-BC **Tomba dei Rilievi**, are decorated with painted reliefs.

Back in Cerveteri, the **Museo Nazionale di Cerveteri** (Piazza Santa Maria; adult/reduced €8/5, incl Necropolis €10/6; ☺8.30am-7.30pm Tue-Sun) displays treasures from the tombs.

Tuscan Wine Tour

4

Tuscany has its fair share of highlights, but few can match the indulgence of a drive through its wine country – an intoxicating blend of scenery, acclaimed restaurants and ruby-red wine.

TRIP HIGHLIGHTS

4 DAYS
148KM / 92 MILES

START
Florence

34 km
Greve in Chianti
Taste Tuscany's best at Greve's vast cellar

4 **3** Panzano in Chianti

Radda in Chianti

Badia a Passignano
Idyllically located wine estate and top restaurant

41 km

Siena

6

67 km
Castello di Ama
Marvel at modern art and Chianti Classico

119 km

Montalcino
A fortified hilltown, home of Brunello di Montalcino

7

FINISH
Montepulciano

GREAT FOR...

BEST TIME TO GO
Autumn for earthy hues and the grape harvest.

ESSENTIAL PHOTO
Panoramas from Montalcino's Fortezza.

BEST FOR GOURMETS
Tuscan *bistecca* (steak) in Panzano in Chianti.

ft Grape harvest, Chianti region

Tuscan Wine Tour

Meandering through Tuscany's bucolic wine districts, this classic Chianti tour offers a taste of life in the slow lane. Once out of Florence (Firenze), you'll find yourself on quiet back roads driving through wooded hills and immaculate vineyards, stopping off at wine estates and hilltop towns to sample the local vintages. En route, you'll enjoy soul-stirring scenery, farmhouse food and some captivating Renaissance towns.

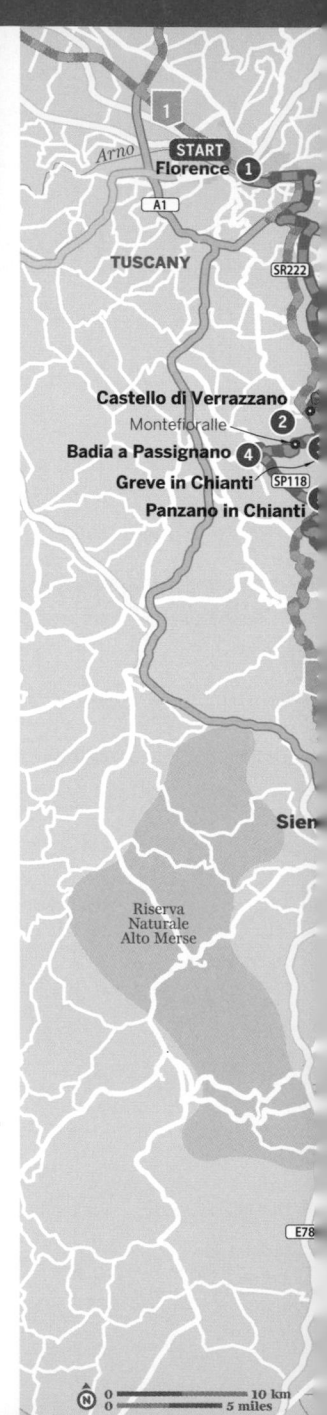

❶ Florence (p56)

Whet your appetite for the road ahead with a one-day cooking course at the **Food & Wine Academy** (☎055 012 39 94; www.florencecookingclasses. com; Via de' Lamberti 1; course with lunch €79), one of Florence's many cookery schools. Once you're done at the stove, sneak out to visit the **Chiesa e Museo di Orsanmichele** (Via dell'Arte della Lana; admission free; ⊙church 10am-5pm daily, museum 10am-5pm Mon), an inspirational 14th-century church and one of Florence's lesser-known gems. Over the river, you can stock up on Tuscan wines and gourmet foods at **Obsequium** (www. obsequium.it; Borgo San Jacopo 17-39r), a well-stocked wine shop on the ground floor of a medieval tower.

The Drive ❯❯ From Florence it's about an hour to Verrazzano. Head south along the scenic SR222 (Via Chiantigiana) towards Greve. When you get to Greti, you'll see a shop selling wine from the Castello di Verrazzano and, just before it, a right turn up to the castle.

❷ Castello di Verrazzano

Some 26km south of Florence, the **Castello di Verrazzano** (☎055 85 42 43; www.verrazzano. com) lords it over a

4 TUSCAN WINE TOUR

220-hectare estate where Chianti Classico, Vin Santo, grappa, honey, olive oil and balsamic vinegar are produced. In a previous life, the castle was home to Giovanni di Verrazzano (1485–1528), an adventurer who explored the North American coast and is commemorated in New York by the Verrazano-Narrows bridge linking Staten Island to Brooklyn.

At the Castello, you can choose from a range of guided tours, including a **Classic Wine Tour** (1½ hours; adult €16; 10am and 3pm Monday to Friday) and **Wine & Food Experience** (three hours, adult €58; noon Monday to Friday), which includes lunch with the estate wines. Book ahead.

The Drive » From the Castello it's a simple 10-minute drive to

LINK YOUR TRIP

1 World Heritage Wonders

Turn your wine tour into a detour from a trip that takes in Italy's big-name cities. (p19).

2 Tuscan Landscapes

Work these two trips together with crossovers at Siena and Montpulciano (p29).

Greve in Chianti. Double back to the SR222 in Greti, turn right and follow for about 3km.

TRIP HIGHLIGHT

❸ Greve in Chianti (p79)

The main town in the Chianti Fiorentino, the northernmost of the two Chianti districts, Greve in Chianti has been an important wine centre for centuries. For a James Bond-esque tasting experience visit **Antinori nel Chianti Classico** (☎0552 35 97 00; www.antinorichianticlassico. it; Via Cassia per Siena 133, Località Bargino; tour & tasting €25-50, bookings essential; ☺10am-6pm summer, to 5pm winter) an exquisitely designed winery full of architectural flourishes and state-of-the-art equipment. Your one-hour guided tour (English and Italian) finishes with a tutored tasting of three Antinori wines beside the family museum. Another family business is the **Antica Macelleria Falorni** (www.

falorni.it; Piazza Matteotti 71; ☺9.30am-1.30pm & 3.30pm-7.30pm Mon-Sat, 10am-1pm Sun) run by the Bencistà Falorni family. It's an atmospheric butcher's shop that they established in the early 18th century and which specialises in delicious picnic-perfect *finocchiona briciolona* (pork salami made with fennel seeds and Chianti wine). The Falorni family also run **Enoteca Falorni** (www.lecantine.it; Piazza delle Cantine 2; ☺10am-7pm), the town's top cellar, where you can sample all sorts of local wines.

The Drive >> From Greve turn off the main through road, Viale Giovanni di Verrazzano, near the Esso petrol station, and head up towards Montefioralle. Continue on as the road climbs past olive groves and through woods to Badia a Passignano, about 15 minutes away.

TRIP HIGHLIGHT

❹ Badia a Passignano

Encircled by cypress trees and surrounded by swaths of olive groves and vineyards, the 11th-century **Badia a Passignano** (Passignano Abbey; ☎055 807 12 78; www.osteriadipassignano. com) sits at the heart of a historic wine estate. It's owned by the Antinoris, one of Tuscany's oldest and most prestigious winemaking families, and offers a range of gastro visits and tours. Guided cellar tours, vineyard visits and cookery courses require a minimum of four people and prior booking, but you can taste and purchase wines and olive oil at **La Bottega** (☺10am-7.30pm Mon-Sat), the estate's wine shop, without a reservation.

The Drive >> From Badia a Passignano, double back towards Greve and pick up the signposted SP118 for a pleasant 3km drive along the narrow tree-shaded road to Panzano.

❺ Panzano in Chianti

The quiet medieval town of Panzano is an essential stop on any gourmet's tour of Tuscany. Here you can stock up on meaty picnic fare at the **Antica Macelleria Cecchini** (www. dariocecchini.com; Via XX Luglio 11; ☺9am-4pm Mon-Thu & Sun, to 6pm Fri & Sat), a celebrated butcher's shop run by the poetry-spouting guru of Tuscan meat, Dario Cecchini. Alternatively, you can

TOP TIP: DRIVING IN CHIANTI

To cut down on driving stress, purchase a copy of *Le strade del Gallo Nero* (€2), a useful map that shows major and secondary roads and has a comprehensive list of wine estates. It's available at Greve in Chianti's **tourist office** (☎055 854 62 99; www.comune.greve-in-chianti.fi.it/ps/s/info-turismo; Piazza Matteotti 11; ☺10am-1pm & 3-7pm Apr-Nov).

TUSCAN REDS

Something of a viticultural powerhouse, Tuscany excites wine buffs with its myriad of full-bodied, highly respected reds. Like all Italian wines, these are classified according to strict guidelines, with the best denominated *Denominazione di Origine Controllata e Garantita* (DOCG), followed by *Denominazione di Origine Controllata* (DOC) and *Indicazione geografica tipica* (IGT).

Chianti

Cheery, full and dry, contemporary Chianti gets the thumbs up from wine critics. Produced in seven subzones from Sangiovese and a mix of other grape varieties, Chianti Classico is the best known, with its Gallo Nero (Black Cockerel) emblem that once symbolised the medieval Chianti League. Young, fun Chianti Colli Senesi from the Siena hills is the largest subzone; Chianti delle Colline Pisane is light and soft in style; and Chianti Rùfina comes from the hills east of Florence.

Brunello di Montalcino

Brunello is up there at the top with Italy's most prized wines. The product of Sangiovese grapes, it must spend at least two years ageing in oak. It is intense and complex with an ethereal fragrance, and is best paired with game, wild boar and roasts. Brunello grape rejects go into Rosso di Montalcino, Brunello's substantially cheaper but wholly drinkable kid sister.

Vino Nobile di Montepulciano

Prugnolo Gentile grapes (a clone of Sangiovese) form the backbone of the distinguished Vino Nobile di Montepulciano. Its intense but delicate nose and dry, vaguely tannic taste make it the perfect companion to red meat and mature cheese.

Super Tuscans

Developed in the 1970s, the Super Tuscans are wines that fall outside the traditional classification categories. As a result they are often made with a combination of local and imported grape varieties, such as Merlot and Cabernet. Sassacaia, Solaia, Bolgheri, Tignanello and Luce are all super-hot Super Tuscans.

eat at one of his three eateries: the **Officina della Bistecca** (☑055 85 21 76; set menu €50; ⏱dinner 8pm Tue, Fri & Sat, lunch 1pm Sun), which serves a simple set menu based on *bistecca*; **Solociccia** (☑055 85 27 27; set menus €30–€50; ⏱sittings 1pm, 7pm & 9pm daily), where guests share a communal table to sample meat dishes other than *bistecca*; and **Dario DOC** (light menu €20;

⏱lunch Mon-Sat), a casual daytime eatery. Book ahead for the Officina and Solociccia.

The Drive » From Panzano, it's about 20 minutes to the Castello di Ama. Strike south on the SR222 towards Radda in Chianti, enjoying views off to the right as you wend your way through the green countryside. At Croce, just beyond Radda, turn left and head towards Lecchi and San Sano. The Castello di Ama is signposted after a further 7km.

TRIP HIGHLIGHT

⑥ Castello di Ama

To indulge in some contemporary-art appreciation between wine tastings, make for the **Castello di Ama** (☑0577 74 60 31; www. castellodiama.com; guided tours €15, with wine & oil tasting €35; ⏱by appointment) near Lecchi. The highly regarded Castello di Ama

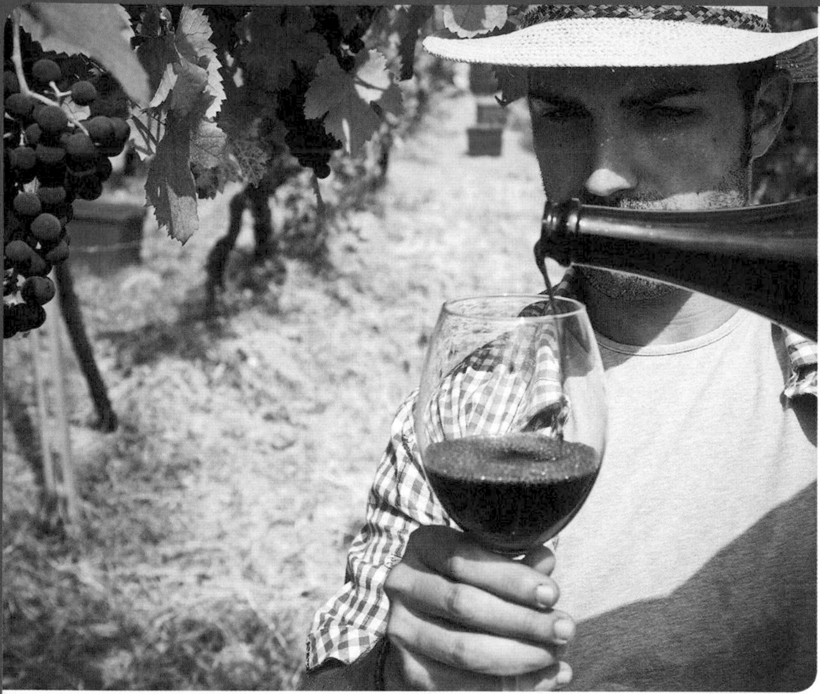

MONTALCINO

BRUNELLO DI MONTALCINO

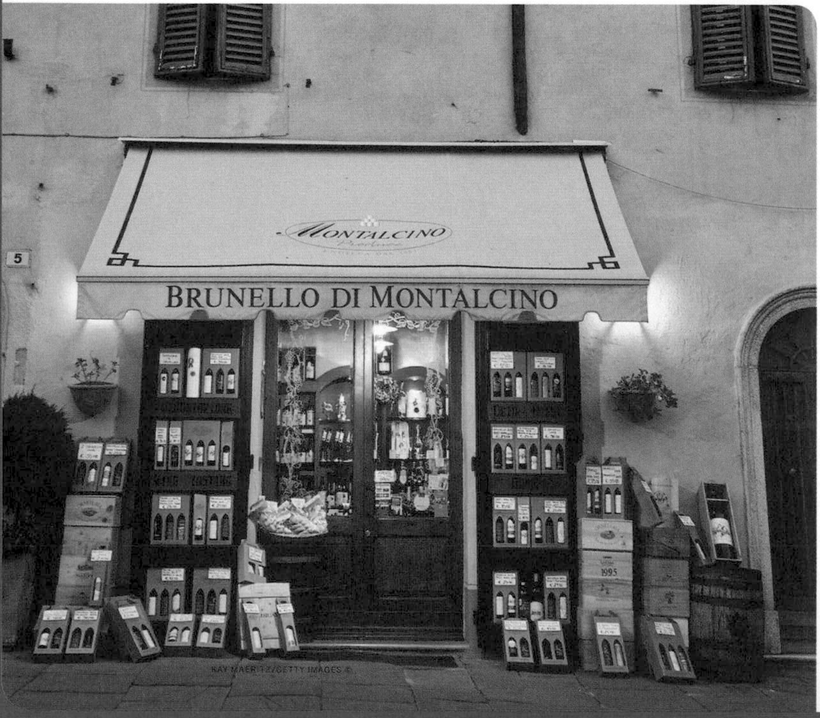

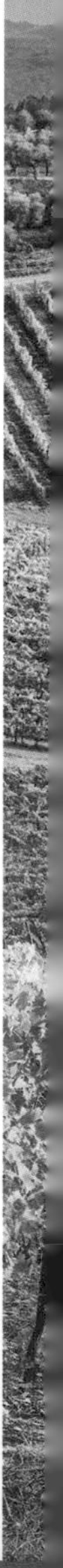

5

1995

estate produces a fine Chianti Classico and has an original sculpture park showcasing 12 site-specific works by artists including Louise Bourgeois, Chen Zhen, Anish Kapoor, Kendell Geers and Daniel Buren. Book ahead.

The Drive » Reckon on about 1½ hours to Montalcino from the Castello. Double back to the SP408 and head south to Lecchi and then on towards Siena. Skirt around the east of Siena and pick up the SR2 (Via Cassia) to Buonconvento and hilltop Montalcino, off to the right of the main road.

- - - - - - - - - - - -

TRIP HIGHLIGHT

❼ Montalcino (p82)

Montalcino, a pretty medieval town perched above the Val d'Orcia, is home to one of Italy's great wines, Brunello di Montalcino (and the more modest, but still very palatable, Rosso di Montalcino). There are plenty of *enoteche* (wine bars) where you can taste and buy, including one in the **Fortezza** (Piazzale Fortezza; adult/child €4/2; ☺9am–8pm summer, shorter hrs winter), the 14th-century fortress that dominates the town's skyline.

For a tasting, head 5km out of town on the road to Grosseto to **Poggio Antico** (☏0577 84 80 44; www.poggioantico. com; ☺cantina 10am-6pm, restaurant noon-2.30pm & 7-9.30pm Tue-Sun, closed Sun

Top left Wine tasting in Chianti
Far left Montalcino wine shop
Left Vineyards near Radda in Chianti (p80)

evening winter). It makes award-winning wines (try its Brunello Altero or Riserva), conducts free cellar tours in Italian, English and German, offers paid tastings (approx €25 depending on wines) and has an on-site restaurant (meals €40). Book tours in advance.

The Drive » From Montalcino, head downhill and then, after about 8km, turn onto the SR2. At San Quirico d'Orcia pick up the SP146, a fabulously scenic road that weaves along the Val d'Orcia through rolling green hills, past the pretty town of Pienza, to Montepulciano. Allow about an hour.

8 Montepulciano (p85)

Set atop a narrow ridge of volcanic rock, the Renaissance centre of Montepulciano produces the celebrated red wine Vino Nobile. For a drop,

head up the main street, called in stages Via di Gracciano nel Corso, Via di Voltaia del Corso and Via dell'Opio nel Corso, to the **Cantine Contucci** (www.contucci.it; Via del Teatro 1; admission free, fee for

---

DETOUR: ABBAZIA DI SANT'ANTIMO

Start: 7 Montalcino

The striking Romanesque **Abbazia di Sant'Antimo** (www.antimo.it; Castelnuovo dell'Abate; admission free; ☺10.15am-12.30pm & 3-6.30pm Mon-Sat, 9.15-10.45am & 3-6pm Sun) lies in an isolated valley just below the village of Castelnuovo dell'Abate, 10.5km from Montalcino.

According to tradition, Charlemagne founded the original monastery in 781. The exterior, built in pale travertine stone, is simple but for the stone carvings, which include various fantastical animals. Inside, study the capitals of the columns lining the nave, especially the one representing Daniel in the lions' den.

Music lovers should try to time their visit to coincide with the daily services, which include Gregorian chants. Check the website for times.

---

tastings; ☺9.30am-12.30pm & 2.30-6pm Mon-Fri, from 9.30am Sat & Sun), housed underneath the *palazzo* (mansion) of the same name. A second cellar, the **Cantina de' Ricci** (☎0578 75 71 66; www. dericci.it; Via Collazzi 7; tasting €6, light lunch plus tasting & guided visit €15; ☺9.30am-6pm), occupies a grotto-like space underneath **Palazzo Ricci** near **Piazza Grande**, the town's highest point.

WINE TASTING GOES HIGH TECH

One of Tuscany's biggest cellars, Enoteca Falorni (p48) stocks more than 2000 labels, of which more than 140 are available for tasting. It's a lovely, brick-arched place, but wine tasting here is a very modern experience, thanks to a sophisticated wine-dispensing system that preserves wine in an open bottle for up to three weeks and allows tasters to serve themselves by the glass. The way it works at the Enoteca Falorni is that you buy a prepaid wine card costing €10 to €25 from the central bar, stick it into one of the many taps and out trickles your tipple of choice. Any unused credit is then refunded when you return the card.

Country road lined with cyprus trees, Montalcino

FRANZ MARC FREI / LOOK-FOTO/GETTY IMAGES ©

Destinations

Florence & Eastern Tuscany (p56)
Florence is a city buzzing with romance and history, set in a region of gently rolling hills, sun-kissed vineyards and avenues of cypress trees.

Siena & Southern Tuscany (p74)
Beautifully preserved, medieval Siena crowns a region that produces some of Italy's most famous wines.

Pisa & Northern Tuscany (p88)
There is more to this green corner of Tuscany than Italy's iconic Leaning Tower.

Rome & Lazio (p98)
No trip through Italy would be complete without a visit to the Eternal City – a place that has dazzled visitors for centuries.

Wine bar, Montalcino (p82)
RICHARD I'ANSON/GETTY IMAGES ©

Life is sweet around leading lady Florence, known for her truly extraordinary treasure trove of world-class art and architecture, and cuisine emulated the world over. Away from the city the pace slows as magnificent landscapes cast their seductive spell.

Florence & Eastern Tuscany

FLORENCE

POP 377,200

Controversy continues over the founding of Florence. Although the most commonly accepted story tells us that Emperor Julius Caesar founded Florentia around 59 BC, there is archaeological evidence of an Etruscan village around 200BC. Over the centuries the city has known many different incarnations under different rulers. The influence of the wealthy Medici family in the 15th century lead to a flowering of art, music and poetry, turning Florence into Italy's cultural capital.

In 1737 Tuscany passed to the French House of Lorraine, which retained control, apart from a brief interruption under Napoleon, until it was incorporated into the Kingdom of Italy in 1860. Florence briefly became the national capital but Rome assumed the mantle permanently in 1870.

👁 Sights

Duomo   CATHEDRAL
(Map p58; Cattedrale di Santa Maria del Fiore; www.operaduomo.firenze.it; Piazza del Duomo; ⏱10am-5pm Mon-Wed & Fri, to 4.30pm Thu, to 4.45pm Sat, 1.30-4.45pm Sun) **FREE** Florence's Duomo is the city's most iconic landmark. Capped by a red-tiled cupola, it's a staggering construction whose breathtaking pink, white and green marble facade and graceful *campanile*

(bell tower) dominate the medieval cityscape. Sienese architect Arnolfo di Cambio began work on it 1296, but construction took almost 150 years and it wasn't consecrated until 1436. In the echoing interior, look out for frescoes by Vasari and Zuccari and look up to 44 stained-glass windows. The **cupola** is a feat of engineering and one that cannot be fully appreciated without climbing its 463 interior stone steps (adult/child incl campanile & baptistry €15/3). It was built between 1420 and 1436 to a design by Filippo Brunelleschi, and is a staggering 91m high and 45.5m wide. The 414-step climb up the cathedral's 85m-tall **campanile**, begun by Giotto in 1334, rewards with a staggering city panorama. The first tier of bas-reliefs around the base of its elaborate Gothic facade are copies of those carved by Pisano depicting the Creation of Man and the *attività umane* (arts and industries).

Piazza della Signoria   MUSEUM
(Map p58; Piazza della Signoria) The hub of local life since the 13th century, Florentines flock here to meet friends and chat over early-evening aperitivi at historic cafes. Presiding over everything is **Palazzo Vecchio**, Florence's city hall, and the 14th-century **Loggia dei Lanzi**, an open-air gallery showcasing Renaissance sculptures, including

Florence

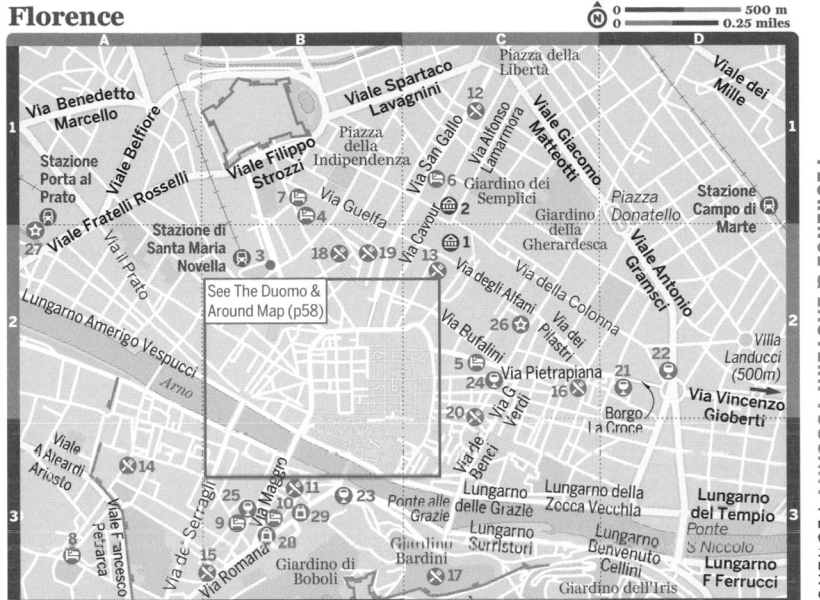

Florence

Giambologna's *Rape of the Sabine Women* (c 1583), Benvenuto Cellini's bronze *Perseus* (1554) and Agnolo Gaddi's *Seven Virtues* (1384–89).

Galleria degli Uffizi GALLERY
(Map p58; Uffizi Gallery; www.uffizi.firenze.it; Piazzale degli Uffizi 6; adult/reduced €8/4, incl temporary exhibition €12.50/6.25; ⊙8.15am-6.50pm

Tue-Sun) Home to the world's greatest collection of Italian Renaissance art, Florence's premier gallery occupies the vast U-shaped Palazzo degli Uffizi, built between 1560 and 1580 to house government offices. The collection, bequeathed to the city by the Medici family in 1743 on condition that it never leave Florence, contains some of Italy's best-known paintings including Piero della

The Duomo & Around

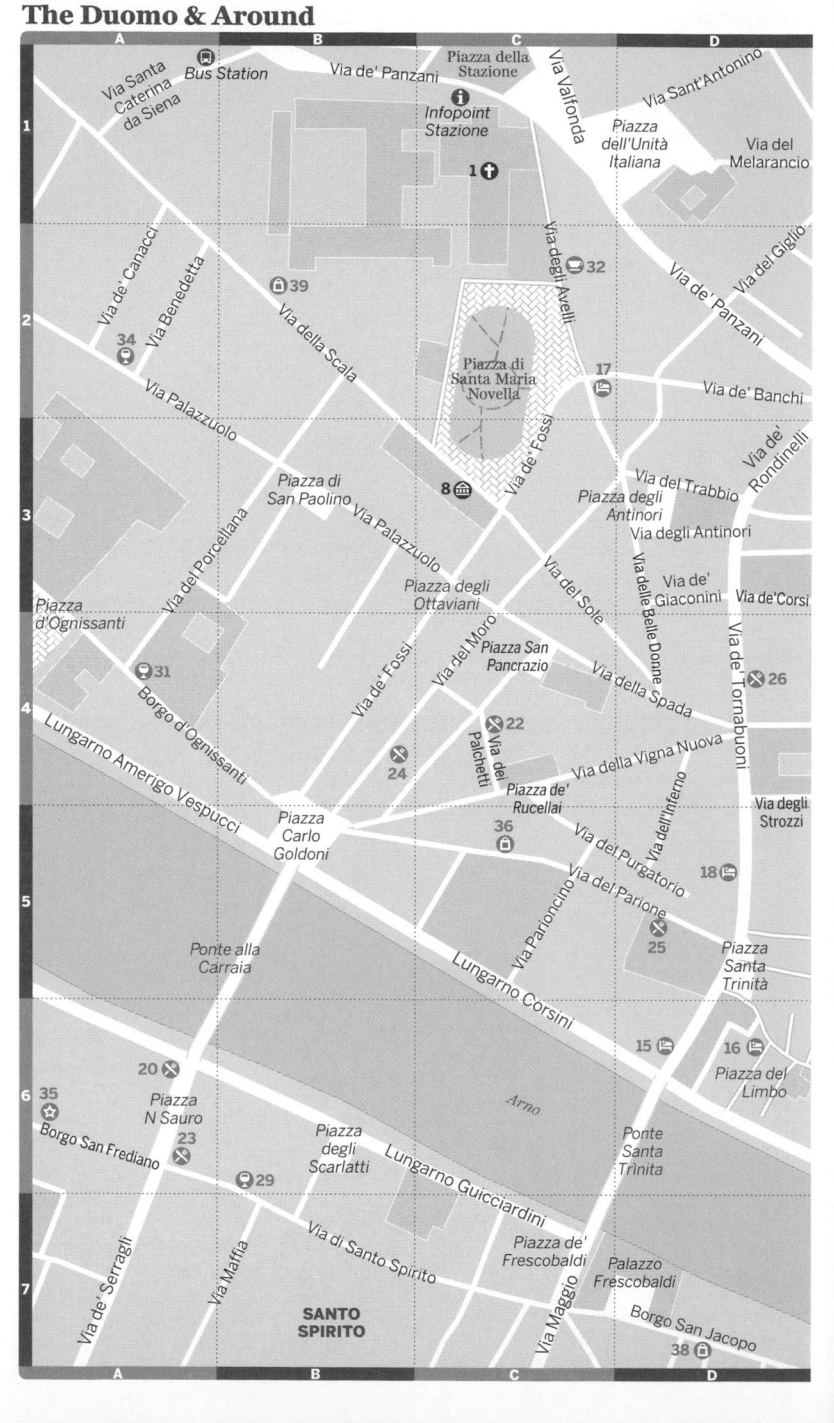

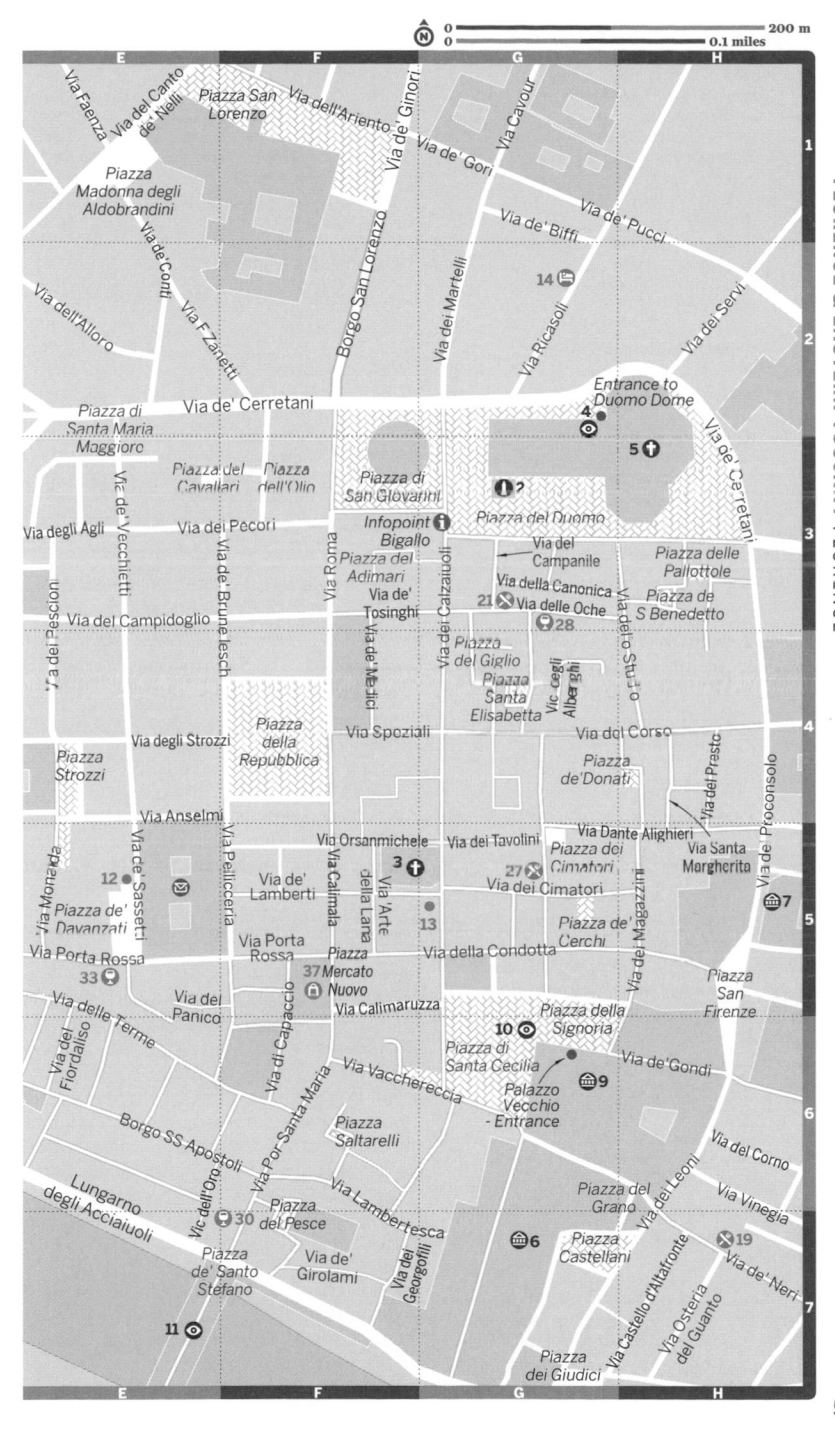

The Duomo & Around

Francesco's profile portaits of the Duke and Duchess of Urbino and room full of masterpieces by Sandro Botticelli.

Chiesa e Museo di Orsanmichele CHURCH, MUSEUM
See p46

Museo del Bargello MUSEUM
(Map p58; www.polomuseale.firenze.it; Via del Proconsolo 4; adult/reduced €4/2; ⊙8.15am-4.50pm summer, to 1.50pm winter, closed 1st, 3rd & 5th Sun & 2nd & 4th Mon of month) Behind the stark walls of Palazzo del Bargello, Florence's earliest public building, the *podestà* meted out justice from the late 13th century until 1502. Today the building safeguards Italy's most comprehensive collection of Tuscan Renaissance sculpture, with some of Michelangelo's best early works and a hall full of Donatello. Michelangelo was just 21 when a cardinal commissioned him to create the drunken, grape-adorned Bacchus (1496-97), displayed in Bargello's downstairs Sala di Michelangelo.

Basilica di Santa Maria Novella CHURCH
(Map p58; www.chiesasantamarianovella.it; Piazza di Santa Maria Novella 18; adult/reduced €5/3.50; ⊙9am-5.30pm Mon-Thu, 11am-5.30pm Fri, 9am-5pm Sat, 1-5pm Sun) The striking green-and-white marble facade of 13th- to 15th-century Basilica di Santa Maria Novella fronts a monastical complex, with romantic church cloisters and a frescoed chapel. The basilica itself is full of artistic masterpieces, climaxing with frescoes by Domenico Ghirlandaio. The lower section of the basilica's striped marbled facade is transitional from Romanesque to Gothic; the upper section and the main doorway (1456-70) were designed by Leon Battista Alberti.

Museo Novecento MUSEUM
(Map p58; Museum of the 20th Century; ☑055 28 61 32; www.museonovecento.it; Piazza di Santa Maria Novella 10; adult/reduced €8.50/4; ⊙10am-6pm Mon-Wed, to 2pm Thu, to 9pm Fri, to 8pm Sat & Sun) Don't allow the Renaissance to distract from Florence's fantastic modern art museum, in a 13th-century *palazzo* (mansion) previously used as a pilgrim shelter, hospital and school. A well-articulated itinerary guides visitors through modern Italian painting and sculpture from the early 20th century to the late 1980s. Installation art makes effective use of the outside space on the 1st-floor loggia. Fashion and theatre get a nod on the 2nd floor, and the itinerary ends with a 20-minute cinematic montage of the best films set in Florence.

Galleria dell'Accademia

GALLERY

(Map p57; www.polomuseale.firenze.it; Via Ricasoli 60; adult/reduced €8/4; ⊗ 8.15am-6.50pm Tue-Sun) A queue marks the door to this gallery, built to house one of the Renaissance's most iconic masterpieces, Michelangelo's *David*. But the world's most famous statue is worth the wait. The subtle detail of it – the veins in his arms, the leg muscles, the change in expression as you move around the statue – *is* impressive.

Museo di San Marco

MUSEUM

(Map p57; www.polomuseale.firenze.it; Piazza San Marco 1; adult/reduced €4/2; ⊗ 8.15am-1.50pm Mon-Fri, 8.15am-4.50pm Sat & Sun, closed 1st, 3rd & 5th Sun & 2nd & 4th Mon of month) At the heart of Florence's university area sits **Chiesa di San Marco** and adjoining 15th-century Dominican monastery where both gifted painter Fra' Angelico (c 1395–1455) and the sharp-tongued Savonarola (1452–1498) piously served God. Today the monastery, aka one of Florence's most spiritually uplifting museums, showcases the work of Fra' Angelico. After centuries of being known as 'Il Beato Angelico' (literally 'The Blessed Angelic One') or simply 'Il Beato' (The Blessed), the Renaissance's most blessed religious painter was made a saint by Pope John Paul II in 1984.

Ponte Vecchio

BRIDGE

(Map p58) Dating to 1345, Ponte Vecchio was the only Florentine bridge to survive destruction at the hands of retreating German forces in 1944. Above the jewellers' shops on the eastern side, the **Corridoio Vasariano** (Vasari corridor) is a 16th-century passageway between the Uffizi and Palazzo Pitti that runs around, rather than through, the medieval **Torre dei Mannelli** at the bridge's southern end. The first evidence of a stone bridge here, at the narrowest crossing point along the entire length of the Arno, dates from 972.

👉 Tours

Food & Wine Academy

TOUR

(Map p58; see p46)

City Sightseeing Firenze

BUS TOUR

(Map p57; ☑ 055 29 04 51; www.firenze.city-sightseeing.it; Piazza della Stazione 1; adult 1/2/3 days €20/25/30) Explore Florence by red open-top bus, hopping on and off at 15 bus stops around the city. Tickets, sold by the driver, are valid for 24 hours.

ArtViva

WALKING TOUR

(Map p58; ☑ 055 264 50 33; www.italy.artviva.com; Via de' Sassetti 1; per person from €25) One- to

three-hour city walks led by historians or art history graduates: tours include the Uffizi, the Original David tour and an adult-only 'Sex, Drugs & the Renaissance' art tour.

✨🎭 Festivals & Events

Festa di Anna Maria Medici

CULTURAL

(⊗ 18 Feb) Florence's Feast of Anna Maria Medici marks the death in 1743 of the last Medici, Anna Maria, with a costumed parade from Palazzo Vecchio to her tomb in the Cappelle Medicee.

Maggio Musicale Fiorentino

PERFORMING ARTS

(www.operadifirenze.it) Italy's oldest arts festival features world-class performances of theatre, classical music, jazz and dance; April to June.

Festa di San Giovanni

RELIGIOUS

(⊗ 24 Jun) Florence celebrates its patron saint, John, with a *calcio storico* (historic football match) on Piazza di Santa Croce and fireworks over Piazzale Michelangelo.

🛏 Sleeping

🛏 Around Piazza del Duomo & Piazza della Signoria

Hotel Cestelli

HOTEL €

(Map p58; ☑ 055 21 42 13; www.hotelcestelli.com; Borgo SS Apostoli 25; d €70-100, without bathroom s €40-60, d €50-80; ⊗ closed 4 weeks Jan-Feb, 2-3 weeks Aug; ☎) Housed in a 12th-

---

> ### ℹ SAVVY ADVANCE PLANNING
>
> ➜ To cut costs, visit on the first Sunday of the month when admission to state museums, including the Uffizi and Galleria dell'Accademia, is free.
>
> ➜ Cut queues by booking tickets in advance for the Uffizi and Galleria dell'Accademia.
>
> ➜ The Uffizi, Galleria dell'Accademia and most other state museums are shut on Monday – the perfect day for visiting the hidden gem of Museo di Orsanmichele.
>
> ➜ Catch contemporary art (for free) on Thursday evening at Palazzo Strozzi.
>
> ➜ Book family-friendly tours and/or art workshops at Palazzo Vecchio and Museo Novecento.

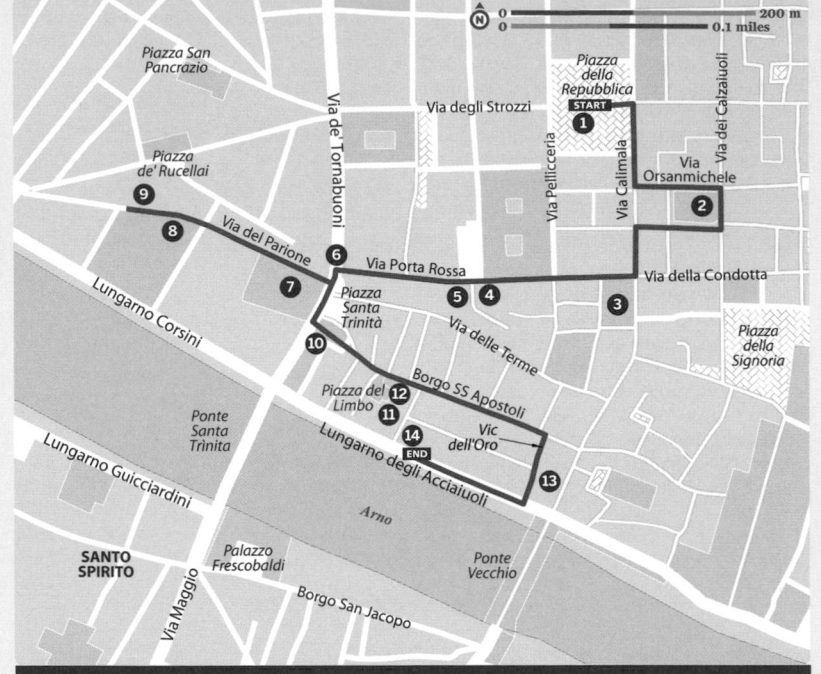

🏃 City Walk
Through the Heart of Florence

START PIAZZA DELLA REPUBBLICA
END AMBLÉ
LENGTH 2KM; TWO HOURS

Start with coffee on **❶ Piazza della Repubblica** then walk one block south along Via Calimala and turn left onto Via Orsanmichele to **❷ Chiesa e Museo di Orsanmichele** (Via dell'Arte della Lana; ⊗ church 10am-5pm, museum 10am-5pm Mon), a unique church with ornate statuary and a fascinating museum. Backtrack to Via Calimala and continue south until you see **❸ Mercato Nuovo** (p74), the 16th-century 'New Market'. Florentines know it as *Il Porcellino* (The Piglet) after the bronze statue of a wild boar on its southern side. Rub its snout to ensure your return to Florence.

Walk past the market and along Via Porta Rossa to **❹ Palazzo Davanzati** (Via Porta Rossa 13; adult/reduced €2/1; ⊗ 8.15am-1.50pm, closed 1st, 3rd & 5th Mon, 2nd & 4th Sun of month) with its magnificent doors and fascinating museum. A few doors down, next to **❺ Slowly** (p73) bar, peep through the sturdy iron gate and look up to admire the ancient brick vaults

of this dark alley – this is hidden Florence of 1001 fabulous doors and lost alleys at its best!

Continue to **❻ Via de' Tornabuoni** with its luxury boutiques. Swoon over **❼ Chiesa di Santa Trinità** (Piazza Santa Trinità; ⊗ 8am-noon & 4-5.45pm Mon-Sat, 8-10.45am & 4-5.45pm Sun), then wander down Via del Parione to visit paper marbler **❽ Alberto Cozzi** (Via del Parione 35r; ⊗ 9am-1pm & 2.30-7pm Mon-Fri, 3-7pm Sat).

Backtrack to Via de' Tornabuoni and turn right, past 13th-century **❿ Palazzo Spini Feroni**, home of Salvatore Ferragamo's flagship store, to Borgo Santissimi Apostoli. A short way ahead on Piazza del Limbo is **⓫ Chiesa dei Santissimi Apostoli**, in a sunken square once used as a cemetery for unbaptised babies.

After browsing Tuscan olive oil in **⓬ La Bottega dell'Olio** (Piazza del Limbo 2r; ⊗ 2.30-6.30pm Mon, 10am-1pm & 2-6.30pm Tue-Sat), continue east and turn right into Vicolo dell' Oro, home to the **⓭ Hotel Continentale**, whose rooftop terrace is the perfect spot for a sundowner with a Ponte Vecchio view. If hipster Florence is more your cup of tea, indulge in an al fresco *aperitivo* at **⓮ Amblé** (☎ 055 26 85 28; Piazzetta dei del Bene 7a; ⊗ 10am-10pm Mon-Sat, noon-10pm Sun).

century *palazzo* a hop from fashionable Via de' Tornabuoni, this intimate eight-room hotel is a gem. Rooms reveal an understated style, tastefully combining polished antiques with spangly chandeliers, vintage art and silk screens. Owners Alessio and Asumi are a mine of local information and are happy to share their knowledge. No breakfast.

Hotel Scoti
PENSION €€

(Map p58; ☎ 055 29 21 28; www.hotelscoti.com; Via de' Tornabuoni 7; s/d €75/130; ☎) Wedged between the designer stores on Florence's smartest shopping strip, this hidden *pensione* is a splendid mix of old-fashioned charm and value for money. Its 16 traditionally styled rooms are spread across the 2nd floor of a towering 16th-century *palazzo*, with some offering lovely rooftop views. The star of the show, though, is the frescoed lounge from 1780. Breakfast €5.

Antica Torre di Via de' Tornabuoni 1
BOUTIQUE HOTEL €€€

(Map p58; ☎ 055 265 81 61; www.tornabuoni1.com; Via de' Tornabuoni 1; d from €200; ☎ ⊕) Just steps from the Arno, inside the beautiful 14th-century Palazzo Gianfigliazzi, is this raved-about hotel. Its 20 rooms are stylish, spacious and contemporary. But what completely steals the show is the stunning rooftop breakfast terrace – easily the best in the city. Sip a cappuccino and swoon over Florence graciously laid out at your feet.

🛏 Santa Maria Novella

Ostello Archi Rossi
HOSTEL €

(Map p57; ☎ 055 29 08 04; www.hostelarchirossi.com; Via Faenza 94r; dm €25-32; ⊙ closed Dec; @ ☎) Guests' paintings and artwork brighten this busy hostel near Santa Maria Novella train station. Bright white dorms have three to nine beds and must be evacuated between 10.30am and 2.30pm for cleaning. Guests can use washing machines, frozen meal dispensers and microwaves. No curfew but guests have to ring the bell after 2am.

Hotel Azzi
HOTEL €€

(Map p57; Locanda degli Artisti; ☎ 055 21 38 06; www.hotelazzi.com; Via Faenza 56/88r; d €120-150, tr €160-180, q €180-210; ❋ ☎) A five-minute walk from the train station adds to the convenience of this 24-room hotel. It's been around a while and furnishings are old-style. But triple and quadruple rooms in particular are enormous – brilliant for families – and the kids' corner with toys in the lounge, library

full of books and summer terrace are welcome touches.

Hotel L'O
DESIGN HOTEL €€€

(Map p58; ☎ 055 27 73 80; www.hotelorologioflorence.com; Piazza di Santa Maria Novella 24; d from €375; ❋ ❋ @ ☎) The type of seductive address that James Bond would feel right at home in, this super-stylish hotel oozes panache. Designed as a showcase for the (very wealthy) owner's (exceedingly expensive) luxury wristwatch collection, L'O (the hip take on its full name, Hotel L'Orologio) has four stars, rooms named after watches and clocks pretty much everywhere. Don't be late...

🛏 San Lorenzo & San Marco

Academy Hostel
HOSTEL €

(Map p58; ☎ 055 239 86 65; www.academyhostel.eu; Via Ricasoli 9r; dm €32-36, s/d €42/100, d without bathroom €85; ❋ @ ☎) This classy 10-room, 40-bed hostel sits on the 1st floor of Baron Ricasoli's 17th-century *palazzo*. The inviting lobby area was once a theatre and 'dorms' sport maximum four or six beds, high moulded ceilings and brightly coloured lockers. The terrace is a perfect spot to chill. No credit cards for payments under €100.

Hotel Orto de' Medici
HOTEL €€

(Map p57; ☎ 055 48 34 27; www.ortodeimedici.it; Via San Gallo 30; d from €184; ❋ @ ☎) This three-star hotel in San Marco redefines elegance with its majestic high ceilings, chic oyster-grey colour scheme and contemporary furnishings, offset to perfection by the historic *palazzo* in which it resides. Hunt down the odd remaining 19th-century fresco, and don't miss the garden complete with lemon trees in terracotta pots and rambling ivy. To really splurge, go for a room with its own flowery terrace.

🛏 Santa Croce

Hotel Dalì
HOTEL €

(Map p57; ☎ 055 234 07 06; www.hoteldali.com; Via dell'Oriuolo 17; d €90, s/d without bathroom €40/70, apt from €95; P ☎) A warm welcome from hosts Marco and Samanta awaits at this lovely small hotel. A stone's throw from the Duomo, it has 10 sunny rooms, some overlooking a leafy inner courtyard, decorated in a low-key modern way and equipped with kettles, coffee and tea. No breakfast, but – miraculous for downtown Florence – free parking in the rear courtyard.

The icing on the cake is a trio of gorgeous self-catering apartments – one with a Duomo view – sleeping two, four or six.

Villa Landucci
B&B €€

(☑055 66 05 95; www.villalanducci.it; Via Luca Landucci 7; d/tr €130/150; P 🕾 🚲) Five elegant and refreshingly spacious rooms are named after Tuscan wines at this gourmet-themed B&B, a short walk away from Santa Croce. The best in the house, 'Bolgheri' and 'Chianti', open onto the well-tended garden with veggie patch, magnolia tree, age-old palm and kids' play area. Breakfast is predominantly organic and free parking is a rarity.

Borrow a bicycle (reserve in advance) to pedal the 500m to Piazza del Duomo. Debora, a sommelier, and partner Matteo, who created the place, are founts of knowledge when it comes to dining well, and they can organise wine-tasting and food tours for guests.

🛏 The Oltrarno

Ostello Tasso
HOSTEL €

(Map p57; ☑055 060 20 87; www.ostellotasso firenze.it; Via Villani 15; dm €30-32, s/d €37/70; @🕾) Hostelling in Florence got a whole load more stylish with the opening of this chic crash pad, a two-minute walk from the tasty eateries of Piazza Tasso. Coloured bed linen and floor rugs give three- to six-bed dorms a boutique charm, the courtyard garden is a dream, and DJs spin tunes in the hip lounge bar (open to nonguests, too). Rates include breakfast, locker, sheets and towel.

Palazzo Guadagni Hotel
HOTEL €€

(Map p57; ☑055 265 83 76; www.palazzogua dagni.com; Piazza Santo Spirito 9; d €150, extra bed €45; ❋🕾) This romantic hotel overlooking Florence's liveliest summertime square is legendary – Zefferelli shot scenes from *Tea with Mussolini* here. Housed in an artfully revamped Renaissance palace, it has 15 spacious if old-fashioned rooms and an impossibly romantic loggia terrace with wicker chairs and predictably dreamy views. Off season, double room rates drop to as low as €90.

SoprArno Suites
GUESTHOUSE €€€

(Map p57; ☑055 046 87 18; www.soprarno suites.com; Via Maggio 35; d from €230; 🕾) A brilliant addition to the hotel scene, this boutique address squirrelled away in an Oltrarno courtyard creates an intimate home-from-home vibe while making it very clear each guest is special. Each of the 11 designer rooms are exquisitely dressed in vintage objets d'art and collectibles – the passion of Florentine owner Matteo and his talented Florence-born, British-raised wife Betty Soldi (herself a calligrapher and graphic designer).

🍴 Eating

Quality ingredients and simple execution are the hallmarks of Florentine cuisine, climaxing with the fabulous *bistecca alla fiorentina,* a huge slab of T-bone steak rubbed with olive oil, seared on the chargrill, garnished with salt and pepper and served *al sangue* (bloody).

TRIPE: FAST-FOOD FAVOURITE

When Florentines fancy a fast munch on the move, they flit by a *trippaio* – a cart on wheels or mobile stand – for a tripe *panino* (sandwich). Think cow's stomach chopped up, boiled, sliced, seasoned and bunged between bread.

Bastions of good old-fashioned Florentine tradition, *trippai* still going strong include the cart on the southwest corner of **Mercato Nuovo** (p69), **L'Antico Trippaio** (Piazza dei Cimatori; ⊙ hours vary), **Pollini** (Piazza Sant'Ambrogio; ⊙ hours vary) and hole-in-the-wall **Da Vinattieri** (Via Santa Margherita 4; panini €4.50; ⊙10am-7.30pm Mon-Fri, to 8pm Sat & Sun). Pay up to €4.50 for a *panino* with tripe doused in *salsa verde* (pea-green sauce of smashed parsley, garlic, capers and anchovies) or garnished with salt, pepper and ground chilli. Alternatively, opt for a bowl (€5.50 to €7) of *lampredotto* (cow's fourth stomach chopped and simmered for hours).

The pew-style seating at staunchly local **Osteria del Cocotrippone** (☑055 234 75 27; Via Vincenzo Gioberti 140; meals €25; ⊙noon-2.30pm & 7-10.30pm) in the off-centre Beccaria neighbourhood is not a coincidence: Florentines come here to venerate the offal side of their city's traditional cuisine. The *trippa alla fiorentina* (tripe in tomato sauce) and *L'Intelligente* (fried brain and zucchini) are local legends.

JOHN FREEMAN/GETTY IMAGES ©

Mercato Centrale (p69)

✖ Piazza del Duomo to Piazza della Signoria

Osteria Il Buongustai OSTERIA €
(Map p58; Via dei Cerchi 15r; meals €15; ⊙ 11.30am-3.30pm Mon-Sat) Run with breathtaking speed and grace by Laura and Lucia, this place is unmissable. Lunchtimes heave with locals who work nearby and savvy students who flock here to fill up on tasty Tuscan homecooking at a snip of other restaurant prices. The place is brilliantly no frills – expect to share a table and pay in cash; no credit cards.

Mariano SANDWICHES €
(Map p58; Via del Parione 19r; panini €3-5; ⊙ 8am-3pm & 5-7.30pm Mon-Fri, 8am-3pm Sat) Our favourite for its simplicity, around since 1973. Sunrise to sunset this brick-vaulted, 13th-century cellar gently buzzes with Florentines propped at the counter sipping coffee or wine or eating salads and *panini*. Come here for a coffee-and-pastry breakfast, light lunch, *aperitivo* or *panino* to eat on the move.

Obicà ITALIAN €€
(Map p58; ☑ 055 277 35 26; www.obica.com; Via de' Tornabuoni 16; 1/2/3 mozzarella €13/20/30,

pizza €9.50-17, taglierini €4.50-19.50, ⊙ noon-4pm & 6.30-11.30pm Mon-Fri, noon-11pm Sat & Sun) Given its exclusive location in Palazzo Tornabuoni, this designer address is naturally ubertrendy – even the table mats are upcycled from organic products. Taste different mozzarella cheeses in the cathedral-like interior or snuggle beneath heaters on sofa seating in the elegant, star-topped courtyard. At *aperitivo* hour nibble on *taglierini* (tasting boards loaded with cheeses, salami, deep fried veg and so on).

✖ Santa Maria Novella

Il Latini TRATTORIA €€
(Map p58; ☑ 055 21 09 16; www.illatini.com; Via dei Palchetti 6r; meals €30; ⊙ 12.30-2.30pm & 7.30-10.30pm Tue-Sun) A veteran guidebook favourite built around traditional *crostini* (toast), Tuscan meats, fine pasta and roasted meats served at shared tables. There are two dinner seatings (7.30pm and 9pm), with service ranging from charming to not so charming. Reservations mandatory.

L'Osteria di Giovanni TUSCAN €€€
(Map p58; ☑ 055 28 48 97; www.osteriadigio vanni.it; Via del Moro 22; meals €50; ⊙ 7-10pm Mon-Fri, noon-3pm & 7-10pm Sat & Sun) Cuisine at

65

Il Porcellino, Mercato Nuovo (p69)

this smart neighbourhood eatery is sumptuously Tuscan. Imagine truffles, tender steaks and pastas such as *pici al sugo di salsiccia e cavolo nero* (thick spaghetti with a sauce of sausage and black cabbage). Throw in a complimentary glass of *prosecco* and you'll want to return time and again.

✕ San Lorenzo & San Marco

Mercato Centrale   TUSCAN €
(Map p57; ✆055 239 97 98; www.mercato centrale.it; Piazza del Mercato Centrale 4; dishes €7-15; ⊙10am-1am, food stalls noon-3pm & 7pm-midnight; 🛜) Meander the maze of stalls crammed with fresh produce at Florence's oldest and largest food market, on the ground of a 19th-century iron-and-glass structure. Then head up to the shiny new 1st floor – a vibrant food fair with dedicated bookshop, cookery school, bar and stalls cooking up steaks, grilled burgers, vegetarian dishes, pizza, gelato, pastries and pasta. Load up and find a free table.

Trattoria Mario   TUSCAN €
(Map p57; www.trattoria-mario.com; Via Rosina 2; meals €20; ⊙noon-3.30pm Mon-Sat, closed 3 weeks Aug) Arrive by noon to ensure a stool around a shared table at this noisy, busy, brilliant trattoria – a legend that retains its soul (and allure with locals) despite being in every guidebook. Charming Fabio, whose grandfather opened the place in 1953, is front of house while big brother Romeo

and nephew Francesco cook with speed in the kitchen.

Antica Trattoria da Tito   TRATTORIA €€
(Map p57; ✆055 47 24 75; www.trattoriadatito.it; Via San Gallo 112r; meals €30; ⊙lunch & dinner Mon-Sat) The 'No well done meat here' sign, strung in the window, says it all: the best of Tuscan culinary tradition is the only thing this iconic trattoria serves. In business since 1913, Da Tito does everything right – tasty Tuscan dishes like onion soup and wild-boar pasta, served with friendly gusto and hearty goodwill to a local crowd. Don't be shy to enter.

✕ Santa Croce

All'Antico Vinaio   OSTERIA €
(Map p58; ✆055 238 27 23; www.allantico vinaio.com; Via dei Neri 65r; tasting platters €8-30, focaccia €5-7; ⊙10am-4pm & 6-11pm Tue-Sat, noon-3.30pm Sun) The crowd spills out the door of this noisy Florentine thoroughbred. Push your way to the tables at the back and pray for a pew to taste cheese and salami in situ. Or join the queue at the deli counter for a well-stuffed focaccia (€5 to €7) wrapped in paper to take away – quality is outstanding. Pour yourself a glass of wine (€2) while you wait.

Il Teatro del Sale   TUSCAN €€
(Map p57; ✆055 200 14 92; www.teatrodelsale. com; Via dei Macci 111r; lunch/dinner/weekend brunch €15/20/30; ⊙11am-3pm & 7.30-11pm Tue-Sat, 11am-3pm Sun, closed Aug) Florentine chef

Fabio Picchi is one of Florence's living treasures who steals the Sant'Ambrogio show with this eccentric, good-value members-only club (everyone welcome, annual membership €7) inside an old theatre. He cooks up weekend brunch, lunch and dinner, culminating at 9.30pm in a live performance of drama, music or comedy arranged by his wife, artistic director and comic actress Maria Cassi.

Dinners are hectic: grab a chair, serve yourself water, wine and antipasti and wait for the chef to yell out what's about to be served before queuing at the glass hatch for your *primo* (first course) and *secondo* (second course). Note this is the only Picchi restaurant to serve pasta! Dessert and coffee are laid out buffet-style just prior to the performance.

✗ The Oltrarno

5 e Cinque   VEGETARIAN €
(Map p57; ☑ 055 274 15 83; Piazza della Passera 1; meals €25; ☺10am-10pm Tue-Sun) The hard work and passion of a photography and antique dealer is behind this highly creative, intimate eating space adored by every savvy local. Cuisine is vegetarian with its roots in Genoa's kitchen – '5 e Cinque' (meaning '5 and 5') is a chickpea sandwich from Livorno and the restaurant's *cecina* (traditional Ligurian flat bread made from chickpea flour) is legendary.

Gnam   BURGERS €
(Map p57; ☑ 055 22 39 52; www.gnamfirenze.it; Via di Carnaldoli 2r; meals from €10; ☺noon-3pm & 6pm-midnight) ✐ Bread arrives at the table in a brown paper bag and fries are served in a miniature copper cauldron at this green, artisanal burger joint in San Frediano. Ingredients are seasonal, locally sourced and organic – and there are vegetarian and gluten-free burgers as well as the traditional beefy variety. Delicous homemade soups also, to eat in or takeway.

Il Santo Bevitore   TUSCAN €€
(Map p58; ☑ 055 21 12 64; www.ilsantobevitore.com; Via di Santo Spirito 64-66r; meals €40; ☺12.30-2.30pm & 7.30-11pm, closed Aug) Reserve or arrive bang on 7.30pm to snag the last table at this ever-popular address, an ode to stylish dining where gastronomes dine by candlelight in a vaulted, whitewashed, bottle-lined interior. The menu is a creative re-invention of seasonal classics, different for lunch and dinner: purple cabbage soup with mozzarella cream and anchovy syrup, acacia

honey bavarese (firm, creamy mousse) with Vin Santo–marinated dried fruits.

La Leggenda dei Frati   TUSCAN €€€
(Map p57; ☑ 055 068 05 45; www.laleggendadeifrati.it; Costa di San Giorgio 6, Villa Bardini; menus €55 & €70, meals €60; ☺lunch & dinner Tue-Sun) This is summer's hottest address. At home in the historic garden house of Villa Bardini, the Legend of Friars (run by the highly regarded Saporito brothers, previously in Castellina in Chianti) enjoys the most romantic terrace with view in Florence. Veggies are plucked fresh from the vegetable patch, which is tucked between waterfalls and ornamental beds in Giardino Bardini, and contemporary art jazzes up the classical interior.

🍷 Drinking & Nightlife

🍸 Piazza del Duomo to Piazza della Signoria

Coquinarius   WINE BAR
(Map p58; www.coquinarius.com; Via delle Oche 11r; crostini & carpacci €4, meals €35; ☺noon-10.30pm) With its old stone vaults, scrubbed wooden tables and refreshingly modern air, this *enoteca* (wine bar) run by the dynamic and charismatic Nicolas is spacious and stylish. The wine list features bags of Tuscan greats and unknowns, and outstanding *crostini* and *carpacci* (cold sliced meats) ensure you don't leave hungry.

La Terrazza   BAR
(Map p58; www.continentale.it; Vicolo dell'Oro 6r; ☺2.30-11.30pm Apr-Sep) This rooftop bar with wooden-decking terrace accessible from the 5th floor of the Ferragamo-owned Hotel Continentale is as chic as one would expect of a fashion-house hotel. Its *aperitivo* buffet is a modest affair, but who cares with that fabulous, drop-dead-gorgeous panorama of one of Europe's most beautiful cities. Dress the part or feel out of place.

Slowly   LOUNGE, BAR
(Map p58; www.slowlycafe.com; Via Porta Rossa 63r; ☺6.30pm-3am Mon-Sat, closed Aug) Sleek and sometimes snooty, this lounge bar with a candle flickering on every table is known for its glam interior, Florentine Lotharios and lavish fruit-garnished cocktails – €10 including buffet during the bewitching *aperitivo* 'hour' (6.30pm to 10pm). Ibiza-style lounge tracks dominate the turntable.

🍷 Santa Maria Novella

Shake Café
CAFE

(Map p58; 📞 055 29 53 10; www.shakecafe.bio; Via degli Avelli 2r; ⊗ 7am-8pm) Handily close to the train station, this self-service juice bar has a perfect people-watching pavement terrace on car-free Piazza Santa Maria Novella. Its juices and smoothies include fabulous combos such as pineapple, fennel, celery, mint, chicory and liquorice. Unusually for Florence, Shake Café also makes cappuccinos with soya, almond or rice milk. Salads, wraps, sandwiches and gelati stave off hunger pangs.

Sei Divino
WINE BAR

(Map p58; Borgo d'Ognissanti 42r; ⊗ 6pm-2am Wed-Mon) This stylish wine bar tucked beneath a red-brick vaulted ceiling is privy to one of Florence's most happening *aperitivo* scenes. It plays music, hosts occasional exhibitions and in summertime the pavement action kicks in. *Aperitivi* 'hour' (with copious banquet) runs 7pm to 10pm.

Space Club
CLUB

(Map p58; www.spaceclubfirenze.com; Via Palazzuolo 37r; admission incl 1 drink €16; ⊗ 10pm-4am) The sheer size of this vast club in Santa Maria Novella impresses – dancing, drinking, video-karaoke in the bar, and a mixed student-international crowd.

🍷 Santa Croce

Kitsch
BAR

(Map p57; www.kitschfirenze.com; Viale A Gramsci 5; ⊗ 6.30pm-2.30am; 🛜) Cent-conscious Florentines love this American-styled bar for its lavish spread at *aperitivi* time – €10 for a drink and sufficient nibbles to not need dinner. It sports a dark-red theatrical interior and a bright 20s- to early-30s crowd out for a good time. DJ sets get the place rocking after dark.

Drogheria
LOUNGE, BAR

(Map p57; www.drogheriafirenze.it; Largo Annigoni 22; ⊗ 10am-2am) Be it rain, hail or shine, this is a lovely contemporary address in Santa Croce. Inside, it is a large space with dark wood furnishings and comfy leaf-green armchairs, perfect for lounging for hours on end. Come spring, the action moves outside onto the terrace, plumb on the huge square across from Sant'Ambrogio market.

Lion's Fountain
IRISH PUB

(Map p57; www.thelionsfountain.com; Borgo degli Albizi 34r; ⊗ 10am-2am) If you have the urge to hear more English than Italian – or local bands play for that matter – this is the place. Plump on a pretty pedestrian square, Florence's busiest Irish pub buzzes in summer when the beer-loving crowd spills across most of the square. Live music.

🍷 The Oltrano

Le Volpi e l'Uva
WINE BAR

(Map p57; www.levolpieluva.com; Piazza dei Rossi 1; ⊗ 11am-9pm Mon-Sat) This unassuming wine bar hidden away by Chiesa di Santa Felicità remains as appealing as the day it opened over a decade ago. Its food and wine pairings are first-class – taste and buy boutique wines by 150 small producers from all over Italy, matched perfectly with cheeses, cold meats and the best *crostini* in town. Wine-tasting classes, too.

Il Santino
WINE BAR

(Map p58; Via di Santo Spirito 60r; ⊗ 12.30-11pm) This pocket-sized wine bar is packed every evening. Inside, squat modern stools contrast with old brick walls, but the real action is outside, from around 9pm, when the buoyant wine-loving crowd spills onto the street.

Volume
BAR

(Map p57; www.volumefirenze.com; Piazza Santo Spirito 3r; ⊗ 9am-1.30am) Armchairs, recycled and upcycled vintage furniture, books to read, juke box, crepes and a tasty choice of nibbles with coffee or a light lunch give this hybrid cafe-bar-gallery real appeal – all in an old hat-making workshop with tools and wooden moulds strewn around. Watch for various music, art and DJ events and happenings.

☆ Entertainment

La Cité
LIVE MUSIC

(Map p58; www.lacitelibreria.info; Borgo San Frediano 20r; ⊗ 8am-2am Mon-Sat, 3pm-2am Sun; 🛜) A hip cafe-bookshop with an eclectic choice of vintage seating, La Cité makes a wonderful, intimate venue for live music – jazz, swing, world music – and book readings.

Jazz Club
JAZZ

(Map p57; Via Nuovo de' Caccini 3; ⊗ 10.30pm-2am Tue-Sat, closed Jul & Aug) Catch salsa, blues, Dixieland and world music as well as jazz at Florence's top jazz venue.

Opera di Firenze OPERA

(Map p57; ☑ 055 277 9350; www.operadifirenze.it; Piazzale Vittorio Gui, Viale Fratelli Rosselli; ⊗ box office 2-6pm Mon, 10am-6pm Tue-Sat) Florence's striking new opera house with contemporary geometric facade sits on the edge of the city park Parco delle Cascine. Its three thoughtfully designed and multifunctional concert halls seat an audience of 5000 and play host to the springtime Maggio Musicale Fiorentino.

🛍 Shopping

Tacky mass-produced souvenirs are everywhere, not least at the city's two main markets, **Mercato Centrale** (www.mercatocentrale.it; Piazza del Mercato Centrale 4; ⊗ 10am-1am, food stalls noon-3pm & 7pm-midnight) and **Mercato Nuovo** (Map p58; Loggia Mercato Nuovo; ⊗ 8.30am-7pm Mon-Sat). But for serious shoppers keen to delve into a city synonymous with craftsmanship since medieval times, there are plenty of workshops and boutiques to visit. Leather goods, jewellery, hand-embroidered linens, designer fashion, perfume, marbled paper, wine, puppets and gourmet foods all make quality souvenirs.

**Officina Profumo-Farmaceutica
di Santa Maria Novella** BEAUTY, GIFTS

(Map p58; www.smnovella.it; Via della Scala 16; ⊗ 9.30am-7.30pm) In business since 1612, this perfumery-pharmacy began life when the Dominican friars of Santa Maria Novella began to concoct cures and sweet-smelling unguents using medicinal herbs cultivated in the monastery garden. The shop today sells a wide range of fragrances, skin-care products, ancient herbal remedies and preparations alongside teas, herbal infusions, liqueurs, scented candles, organic olive oil, chocolate, honey and cookies.

Obsequium FOOD

See p46

& Company ARTS, CRAFTS

(Map p57; http://andcompanyshop.tumblr.com/; Via Maggio 60r; ⊗ 10.30am-1pm & 3-6.30pm Mon-Sat) This Pandora's box of beautiful objects and paper creations is the love child of Florence-born, British-raised calligrapher and graphic designer Betty Soldi and her vintage-loving husband, Matteo Perduca. Together the pair have created an extraordinary boutique showcasing their own customised cards and upcycled homewares alongside work by other designers. Souvenir shopping at its best!

Letizia Fiorini GIFTS, HANDICRAFTS

(Map p58; Via del Parione 60r; ⊗ 10am-7pm Tue-Sat) This charming shop is a one-woman affair – Letizia Fiorini sits at the counter and makes her distinctive puppets by hand in between assisting customers. You'll find Pulcinella (Punch), Arlecchino the clown, beautiful servant girl Colombina, Doctor Peste (complete with plague mask), cheeky Brighella, swashbuckling Il Capitano and many other characters from traditional Italian puppetry.

Giulio Giannini e Figlio HANDICRAFTS

(Map p57; www.giuliogiannini.it; Piazza dei Pitti 37r; ⊗ 10am-7pm Mon-Sat, 11am-6.30pm Sun) This quaint old shopfront has watched Palazzo Pitti turn pink with the evening sun since 1856. One of Florence's oldest artisan families, the Gianninis – bookbinders by trade – make and sell marbled paper, beautifully bound books, stationery and so on. Don't miss the workshop upstairs.

PARKING IN FLORENCE

There is a strict Limited Traffic Zone (ZTL) in Florence's historic centre between 7.30am and 7.30pm Monday to Friday and 7.30am to 6pm Saturday for all nonresidents, monitored by cyclopean cameras positioned at all entry points. The exclusion also applies on Thursday, Friday and Saturday nights from 11pm to 3am late May to mid-September. Motorists staying in hotels within the zone are allowed to drive to their hotel to drop off luggage, but must tell reception their car registration number and the time they were in no-cars-land (there's a two-hour window) so that the hotel can inform the authority and organise a permit. If you transgress, a fine of around €150 will be sent to you (or the car-hire company you used). For more information see www.comune.fi.it.

There is free street parking around Piazzale Michelangelo and plenty of car parks costing between €2 and €3 per hour around town, including at Santa Maria Novella train station, by Fortezza da Basso and in the Oltrarno beneath Piazzale di Porta Romana. Find a complete list of car parks on www.firenzeparcheggi.it.

ⓘ Information

EMERGENCY

Police Station (Questura; ⌨ English-language service 055 497 72 68, 055 4 97 71; http://questure.poliziadistato.it; Via Zara 2; ◷24hr) Should you have a theft or other unfortunate incident to report, the best time to visit the city's police station is between 9am and 2pm weekdays when the foreign-language service – meaning someone speaks who English – kicks in.

MEDICAL SERVICES

24-Hour Pharmacy (Stazione di Santa Maria Novella) This pharmacy inside Florence's central train station opens 24 hours. There is usually at least one member of staff who speaks English.

Dr Stephen Kerr: Medical Service (⌨ 055 28 80 55, 335 8361682; www.dr-kerr.com; Piazza Mercato Nuovo 1; ◷3-5pm Mon-Fri, or by appointment 9am-3pm Mon-Fri) Resident British doctor.

Hospital (Ospedale di Santa Maria Nuova; ⌨ 055 2 75 81; Piazza di Santa Maria Nuova 1)

TOURIST INFORMATION

Airport Tourist Office (⌨ 055 31 58 74; www.firenzeturismo.it; Via del Termine, Aeroporto Vespucci; ◷9am-7pm Mon-Sat, to 2pm Sun)

Infopoint Stazione (⌨ 055 21 22 45; www.firenzeturismo.it; Piazza della Stazione 5; ◷9am-7pm Mon-Sat, to 2pm Sun)

Central Tourist Office (⌨ 055 29 08 32; www.firenzeturismo.it; Via Cavour 1r; ◷9am-6pm Mon-Sat)

ⓘ Getting There & Around

CAR & MOTORCYCLE

Florence is connected by the A1 northwards to Bologna and Milan, and southwards to Rome and Naples. The A11 links Florence with Pistoia, Lucca, Pisa and the coast, but most locals use the FI-PI-LI dual carriageway. Another dual carriageway, the S2, links Florence with Siena.

AIR

Tuscany's main international airport is in Pisa (p121) and offers flights to most major European cities.

Florence Airport (Aeroport Vespucci; ⌨ 055 306 13 00; www.aeroporto.firenze.it; Via del Termine) Also known as Amerigo Vespucci or Peretola airport, 5km northwest of the city centre; domestic and European flights.

BICYCLE & SCOOTER

Milleunabici (www.bicifirenze.it; Piazza della Stazione; 1hr/5hr/1 day €2/5/10; ◷10am-7pm Mar-Oct) Violet bikes to rent in front of Stazione di Santa Maria Novella; leave ID as a deposit.

Florence by Bike (www.florencebybike.com; Via San Zanobi 54r; 1hr/5hr/1 day €3/9/14; ◷9am-1pm & 3.30-7.30pm Mon-Sat, 9am-5pm Sun summer, closed Sun winter) Top-notch bike shop with bike rental (city, mountain, touring and road bikes), itinerary suggestions and organised bike tours (two-hour photography tours of the city by bike, and day trips to Chianti).

PUBLIC TRANSPORT

Buses and electric minibuses run by public transport company ATAF serve the city. Most buses start/terminate at the bus stops opposite the southeastern exit of Stazione di Santa Maria Novella. Tickets valid for 90 minutes (no return journeys) cost €1.20 (€2 on board) and are sold at kiosks, tobacconists and at the **ATAF ticket & information office** (⌨ 199 10 42 45, 800 42 45 00; www.ataf.net; Piazza della Stazione, Stazione di Santa Maria Novella; ◷6.45am-8pm Mon-Sat) inside the main ticketing hall at Santa Maria Novella train station.

A travel pass valid for 1/3/7 days costs €5/12/18. Upon boarding, time-stamp your ticket (punch on board) or risk an on-the-spot €50 fine. One tramline is up and running; more are meant to follow in 2017.

TAXI

Pick one up at the train station or call ⌨ 055 42 42.

EASTERN TUSCANY

The eastern edge of Tuscany is beloved by film directors who've immortalised its landscape and medieval hilltop towns in several critically acclaimed and visually splendid films. Yet the region remains refreshingly bereft of tourist crowds and offers uncrowded trails for those savvy enough to explore here.

Arezzo

POP 99,232

Arezzo may not be a Tuscan centrefold, but those parts of its historic centre that survived merciless WWII bombings are compelling – the city's central square is as beautiful as it appears in Roberto Benigni's classic film *La vita è bella* (Life is Beautiful).

Today, the city is known for its churches, museums and fabulously sloping **Piazza Grande**, across which a huge antiques fair spills during the first weekend of each month. Come dusk, the Arentini (locals of Arezzo)

Arezzo

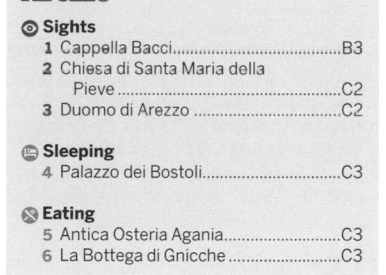

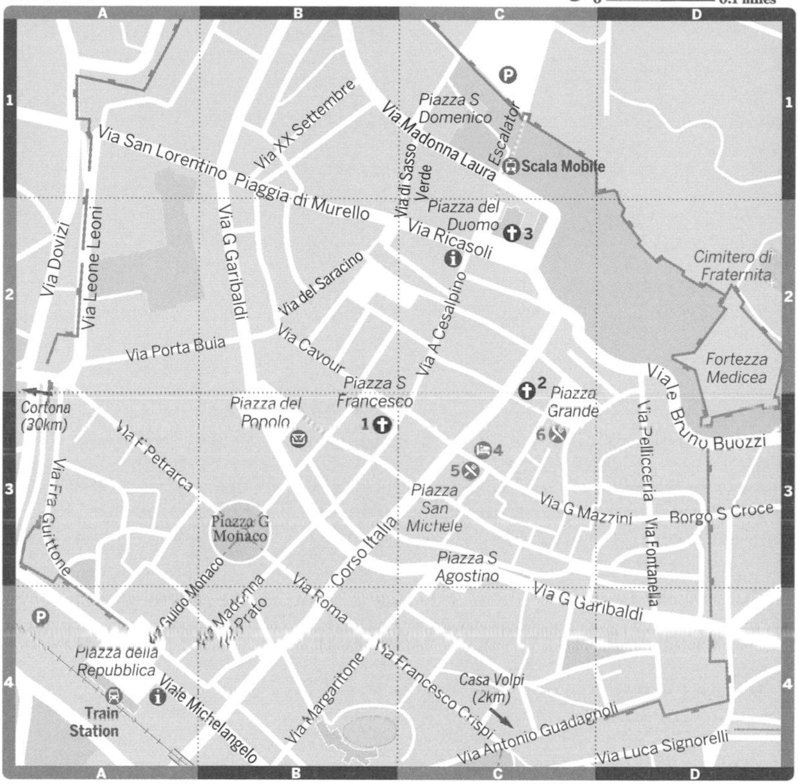

spill along the length of shop-clad Corso Italia for the ritual *passeggiata* (evening stroll).

Sights

Cappella Bacci CHURCH

(☎ 0575 35 27 27; www.pierodellafrancesca.it; Piazza San Francesco; adult/reduced €8/5; ⏲ 9am-6.30pm Mon-Fri, to 5.30pm Sat, 1-5.30pm Sun) This chapel, in the apse of 14th-century Basilica di San Francesco, safeguards one of Italian art's greatest works: Piero della Francesca's fresco cycle of the Legend of the True Cross. Painted between 1452 and 1466, it relates the story of the cross on which Christ was crucified. Only 25 people are allowed in every half-hour, making advance booking (by telephone or email) essential in high season. The ticket office is down the stairs by the basilica's entrance.

Chiesa di Santa Maria della Pieve CHURCH

(Corso Italia 7; ⏲ 8am-12.30pm & 3-6.30pm) FREE This 12th-century church – Arezzo's oldest – has an exotic Romanesque arcaded facade

Arezzo

Sights

1 Cappella Bacci B3
2 Chiesa di Santa Maria della Pieve C2
3 Duomo di Arezzo C2

Sleeping

4 Palazzo dei Bostoli C3

Eating

5 Antica Osteria Agania C3
6 La Bottega di Gnicche C3

adorned with carved columns, each uniquely decorated. Above the central doorway are 13th-century carved reliefs called *Cyclo dei Mesi* representing each month of the year. The plain interior's highlight – removed for restoration work at the time of writing – is Pietro Lorenzetti's polyptych *Madonna and Saints* (1320–24), beneath the semidome of the apse. Below the altar is a 14th-century

silver bust reliquary of the city's patron saint, San Donato.

Duomo di Arezzo
CATHEDRAL

(Cattedrale di SS Donato e Pietro; Piazza del Duomo; ⊙7am-12.30pm & 3-6.30pm) FREE Construction started in the 13th century but Arezzo's cathedral wasn't completed until the 15th century. In the northeast corner, left of the intricately carved main altar, is an exquisite fresco of *Mary Magdalene* (c 1459) by Piero della Francesca. Also notable are five glazed terracottas by Andrea della Robbia and his studio. Behind the cathedral is the pentagonal **Fortezza Medicea** (1502) atop the crest of one of Arezzo's two hills – the *duomo* was built on the crest of the other.

Festivals & Events

Fiera Antiquaria di Arezzo
ANTIQUES

(Arezzo Antique Fair) Tuscany's most famous antiques fair is held in Piazza Grande on the first Sunday and preceding Saturday of every month.

Sleeping

Palazzo dei Bostoli
B&B €

(☑334 1490558; www.palazzobostoli.it; Via G Mazzini 1; s/d €55/75; ❄️🛜) This old-fashioned place offers five simple but comfortable rooms on the 2nd floor of a 13th-century *palazzo* near Piazza Grande. Breakfast – coffee and *cornetto* (croissant) – is served at a bar on nearby Corso Italia.

Casa Volpi
HOTEL €

(☑0575 35 43 64; www.casavolpi.it; Via Simone Martini 29; s/d €65/95; 🅿️@🛜♿) This 18th-century manor is a delicious 1.5km bicycle ride away from the cobbled streets of downtown Arezzo (the hotel lends wheels to guests). Its 15 rooms are decorated in a clasical style, with enough original features – beamed ceilings, red-brick flooring, parquet – to charm. Family-run, the hotel restaurant spills in to the pretty garden in summer. Breakfast €9.

Eating

Antica Osteria Agania
TUSCAN €

(☑0575 29 53 81; www.agania.com; Via G Mazzini 10; meals €25; ⊙noon-3pm & 6-10.30pm Tue-Sun) Agania has been around for years and her fare is die-hard traditional – the tripe and *grifi con polenta* (lambs' cheeks with polenta) are sensational. But it is timeless, welcoming addresses like this, with potted fresh herbs on the doorstep, that remain the cornerstone of Tuscan dining. Begin

with *antipasto misto* (mixed appetisers) followed by your choice of six pastas and eight sauces.

Agania's *pici* (fat spaghetti) with wild-boar sauce is legendary. Arrive by 1pm to beat the crowd of regulars or join the crowd waiting outside.

La Bottega di Gnicche
SANDWICHES €

(www.bottegadignicche.com; Piazza Grande 4; panini €3.50-5; ⊙11am-8pm Thu-Tue) Choose from a delectable array of artisan meats and cheese to stuff in a *panini* at this old-fashioned *alimentari* (grocery store) on Arezzo's main piazza. Eat next to canary-yellow bags of artisan Martelli pasta stacked up on the front porch, or perch on a stool inside.

ℹ Information

Tourist Office (☑0575 40 19 45; www. benvenutiadarezzo.it; Palazzo Comunale, Via Ricasoli; ⊙10am-1pm & 2-7pm Mon-Fri, 10am-1pm Sat & Sun Jun-Sep, to 4pm Oct-May) Find a **branch** (Piazza della Repubblica 22-23; ⊙10.30am-12.30pm & 2-4pm) of the tourist office to the right as you exit the train station.

Una Vetrina per Arezzo e Le Sue Vallate (☑0575 182 27 70; ⊙9am-7pm) Private tourist office on the *scala mobile* leading up to Piazza del Duomo; toilet facilities (€0.50).

Cortona

POP 22,607

Rooms with a view are the rule rather than the exception in this spectacularly sited hilltop town. In the late 14th century Fra' Angelico lived and worked here, and fellow artists Luca Signorelli and Pietro da Cortona were both born within the walls – all are represented in the Museo Diocesano's collection.

◉ Sights

Museo Diocesano
MUSEUM

(Piazza del Duomo 1; adult/reduced €5/3; ⊙10am-7pm Tue-Sun summer, to 5pm Tue-Sun winter) Little is left of the original Romanesque character of Cortona's cathedral, rebuilt several times in a less-than-felicitous fashion. Fortunately, its wonderful artworks have been saved and displayed in this museum. Highlights include a moving *Crucifixion* (1320) by Pietro Lorenzetti and two beautiful works by Fra' Angelico: *Annunciation* (1436) and *Madonna with Child and Saints* (1436–37). Room 1 features a remarkable Roman sarcophagus decorated with a frenzied battle scene between Dionysus and the Amazons.

✿ Festivals & Events

Giostra dell'Archidado   CULTURAL
(www.giostraarchidado.com; ☉ May or Jun) A full
week of medieval merriment (the date varies
to coincide with Ascension Day) culminates
in a crossbow competition.

Cortonantiquaria   FAIR
(www.cortonantiquaria.it; ☉ late Aug or early Sep)
Cortona's well-known antiques market sets
up in the beautiful 18th-century halls of
Palazzo Vagnotti.

🛏 Sleeping

Casa Chilenne   B&B €
(🖉 0575 60 33 20; www.casachilenne.com; Via
Nazionale 65; d €110; ❋ @ 🖥 🛗) Run by San
Franciscan Jeanette and her Cortonese husband Luciano, this welcoming B&B scales a
narrow townhouse on Cortona's main pedestrian street. Five spacious rooms have
access to a small rooftop terrace, complete
with bijou cooking area and chairs to lounge
on. Breakfast is a feast, served around beautifully dressed tables.

La Corte di Ambra   B&B €€
(🖉 0575 178 82 66; www.cortonaluxuryrooms.com;
Via Benedetti 23; d €150-300; ❋ @ 🖥) Squirrelled away in Palazzo Fierli-Petrella, this
contemporary guesthouse has five luxurious
rooms with whitewashed beamed ceilings,
chandelier lighting and beautiful linens in
mellow neutral tones. En suite bathrooms are
up-to-the-minute and – unusually for a Renaissance Tuscan palace – the B&B has a lift;
one room is genuinely wheelchair-friendly.

🍴 Eating & Drinking

Pasticceria Banchelli   PASTRIES €
(🖉 0575 60 10 52; Via Nazionale 11; ☉ 10am-8pm
Tue-Sun) For sinful cakes with coffee, this cake
shop has been the place to go since 1930.

Fiaschetteria La Fett'unta   TUSCAN €
(🖉 0575 63 05 82; www.winebarcortona.com; Via
Giuseppe Maffei 3; meals €15) This tiny, deli-
style *fiaschetteria* (wine seller) with tempting cold cuts and pre-prepared dishes sitting
beneath glass, begging to be gobbled up,
cooks up first-class budget dining. Service is
overwhelmingly friendly, there's a kids' corner, and traditional Tuscan cuisine – fresh
from the kitchen of big sister Osteria del Teatro across the street – is spot on.

Cortona
BRIAN A JACKSON/SHUTTERSTOCK ©

La Bucaccia   TUSCAN €€
(🖉 0575 60 60 39; www.labucaccia.it; Via Ghibellina
17; meals €32, set tasting menu €29; ☉ 12.45-3pm
& 7-10.30pm Tue-Sun) Cortona's finest address,
this gourmet gem is at home in the old medieval stable of a Renaissance *palazzo*. Cuisine
is Tuscan and Cortonese – much meat and
handmade pasta (chestnut ravioli!) – and
the cheese course is superb, thanks to owner
Romano Magi who ripens his own. Dedicated gourmets won't be able to resist the six
pecorino types to taste with fruit sauces, sal-
sas and honeys.

ℹ Information

Tourist Office (🖉 0575 63 72 21; www.
comunedicortona.it; Piazza Signorelli; ☉ 9am-
12.30pm Mon, Wed & Fri, 9am-12.30pm &
3-5.30pm Tue & Thu)

Siena & Southern Tuscany

There's more to central Tuscany than rolling hills, sun-kissed vineyards and avenues of cypress trees. The real gems are the historic towns and cities, most of which are medieval and Renaissance time capsules magically transported to the modern day.

SIENA

POP 54,126

The rivalry between historic adversaries Siena and Florence continues to this day, and participation isn't limited to the locals – most travellers tend to develop a strong preference for one town over the other.

Legend tells us that Siena was founded by the son of Remus, and the symbol of the wolf feeding the twins Romulus and Remus is as ubiquitous in Siena as it is in Rome. In reality the city was probably of Etruscan origin, although it didn't begin to grow into a proper town until the 1st century BC, when the Romans established a military colony here called Sena Julia.

A plague outbreak in 1348 killed two-thirds of Siena's 100,000 inhabitants and led to a period of decline. This culminated in the city being handed over to Cosimo I de' Medici, who barred the inhabitants from operating banks and thus severely curtailed its power.

This centuries-long economic downturn in the wake of the Medici takeover was a blessing in disguise, as the lack of funds meant that Siena was subject to very little redevelopment or new construction. This led to the historic centre's inclusion on Unesco's World Heritage List, as it is the living embodiment of a medieval city.

◉ Sights

Piazza del Campo   FOUNTAIN
See p22; p30

Palazzo Pubblico   HISTORIC BUILDING
See p22; p30

Museo Civico   MUSEUM
(Palazzo Comunale, Piazza del Campo; adult/reduced €9/8; ⊙10am-7pm summer, to 6pm winter) Siena's most famous museum occupies rooms richly frescoed by artists of the Sienese school. Commissioned by the governing body of the city, rather than by the Church, many depict secular subjects. The highlight is Simone Martini's celebrated *Maestà* (Virgin Mary in Majesty; 1315) in the Sala del Mappamondo (Hall of the World Map). It features the Madonna beneath a canopy surrounded by saints and angels, and is Martini's first known work.

Duomo   CATHEDRAL
(www.operaduomo.siena.it; Piazza del Duomo; summer/winter €4/free, when floor displayed €7; ⊙10.30am-7pm Mon-Sat, 1.30-6pm Sun summer, to 5.30pm winter) Siena's cathedral is one of Italy's most awe-inspiring churches. Construction started in 1215 and over the centuries many of Italy's top artists have contributed: Giovanni Pisano designed the white, green and red marble facade; Nicola Pisano carved the elaborate pulpit; Pinturicchio painted some of the

frescoes; Michelangelo, Donatello and Gian Lorenzo Bernini all produced sculptures.

Complesso Museale Santa Maria della Scala
BUILDING

(www.santamariadellascala.com; Piazza del Duomo 1; adult/reduced €9/8; ⏱10.30am-6.30pm Wed-Mon summer, to 4.30pm winter) This former hospital, parts of which date from the 13th century, was built as a hospice for pilgrims travelling the Via Francigena pilgrimage trail. Its highlight is the upstairs Pellegrinaio (Pilgrim's Hall), with vivid 15th-century frescoes by Lorenzo Vecchietta, Priamo della Quercia and Domenico di Bartolo lauding the good works of the hospital and its patrons.

Pinacoteca Nazionale
GALLERY

(Via San Pietro 29; adult/reduced €4/2; ⏱8.15am-7.15pm Tue-Sat, 9am-1pm Sun & Mon) An extraordinary collection of Gothic masterpieces from the Sienese school sits inside the once grand but now sadly dishevelled 14th-century Palazzo Buonsignori. The pick of the collection is on the 2nd floor, including magnificent works by Duccio di Buoninsegna, Simone Martini, Niccolò di Segna, Lippo Memmi, Ambrogio and Pietro Lorenzetti, Bartolo di Fredi and Taddeo di Bartolo.

👉 Tours

Centro Guide Turistiche Siena e Provincia
CULTURAL TOUR

(📞0577 4 32 73; www.guidesiena.it; Galleria Odeon, Via Banchi di Sopra 31; ⏱10am-1pm &

3-5pm Mon-Fri) The pick of the tours offered by this association of accredited guides are the 90-minute Classical Siena Walking Tour (€20, 11am Monday to Saturday), which features key historical and cultural landmarks, and the 90-minute Secret Siena Walk (€20, 11am Sunday), which takes in both Siena's streets and the duomo's crypt. Prices include admission fees.

⭐ Festivals & Events

Accademia Musicale Chigiana
MUSIC

(www.chigiana.it) The Accademia Musicale Chigiana presents three highly regarded concert series featuring classical musicians from around the world: Micat in Vertice from November to April, Settimana Musicale Senese in July, and Estate Musicale Chigiana in July and August.

🛏 Sleeping

Hotel Alma Domus
HOTEL **❶**

(📞0577 4 41 77; www.hotelalmadomus.it; Via Camporegio 37; s €40-52, d €60-€122; ❇️📶🛗) Your chance to sleep in a convent: Alma Domus is owned by the church and is still home to Dominican nuns. The economy rooms are supremely comfortable, and are styled very simply. But the superior ones are sumptuous, with pristine bathrooms, pared-down furniture and bursts of magenta and lime. Many have mini-balconies with views of the *duomo*.

Historic centre, Siena

Siena

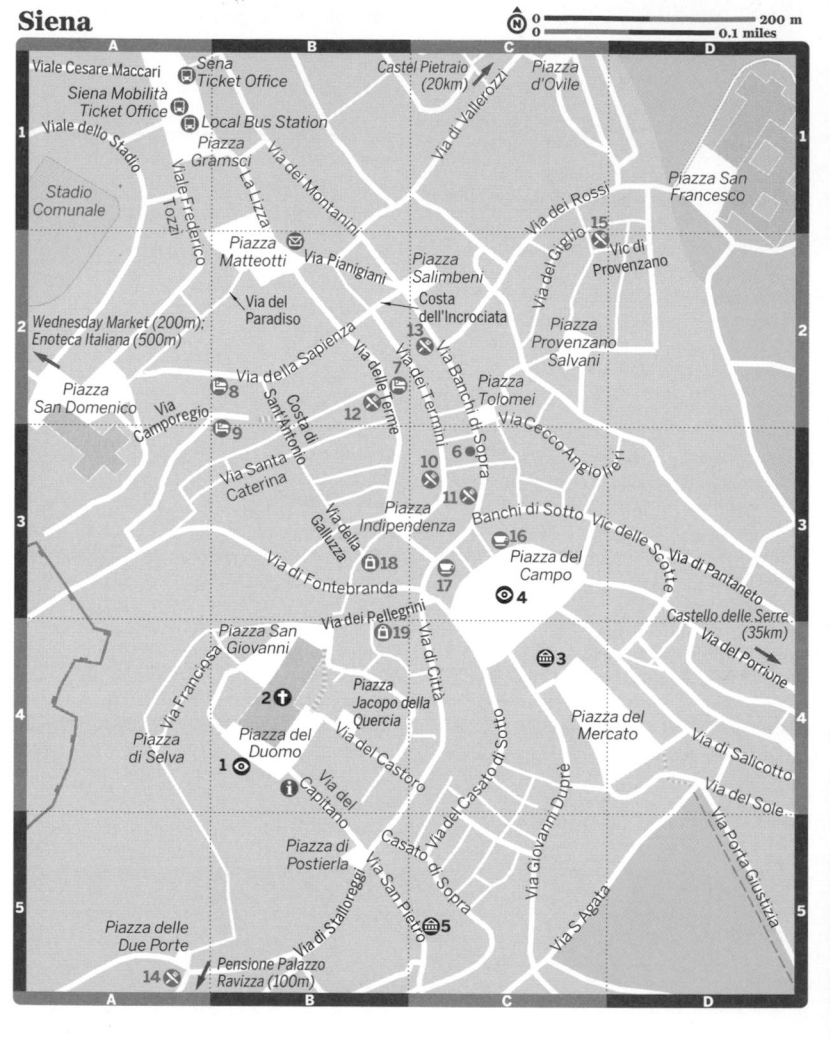

Antica Residenza Cicogna
B&B €

(☎ 0577 28 56 13; www.anticaresidenzacicogna. it; Via delle Terme 76; s €70-95, d €95-115, ste €120-155; ✳ @ 🛜) You get a true feel for Siena's history in this exquisite 13th-century *palazzo* (mansion). Tiled floors, ornate lights and painted ceilings meet tones of yellow ochre and (suitably) burnt sienna. The best of the fabulous suites is named after landscape painter Paesaggi, where bucolic views sit in panels above your head, and a tiny blue passageway winds to the bathroom.

Pensione Palazzo Ravizza
BOUTIQUE HOTEL €€

(☎ 0577 28 04 62; www.palazzoravizza.it; Pian dei Mantellini 34; d €80-220, ste €180-320; P ✳ @ 🛜) Heritage features and luxurious flourishes combine at this Renaissance *palazzo* to create an irresistible hotel. Frescoed ceilings and stone staircases meet elegant furnishings, wooden shutters and (from some bedrooms) captivating views. The greenery-framed rear garden is utterly delightful; settle down in a wicker chair here, gaze out at the hills and you may never want to leave.

Siena

Castel Pietraio   HISTORIC HOTEL €€

(☑ 0577 30 00 20; www.castelpietraio.it; Strada di Strove 33, Monteriggion; s €90, d €120-165) Castel Pietraio is a sleep spot that's simply too good to miss. The medieval castle is owned by Barone Neri Del Nero and bedrooms, in the adjoining outbuildings, are rich in aristocratic trappings with Carrara-marble bathrooms and chestnut beams. The wine cellar, meanwhile, is stocked with the Baron's own DOCG Chianti and DOC Vin Santo. It's 15km west of Siena.

Campo Regio Relais   BOUTIQUE HOTEL €€€

(☑ 0577 22 20 73; www.camporegio.com; Via della Sapienza 25; d €220-400, ste €450; ❄ 🖥) The decor in each of the six, individually styled rooms here is exquisite – expect anything from old mahogany to fine linen, 18th-century antiques to art nouveau. Breakfast is served in the sumptuously decorated lounge or on the terrace, with a sensational view across higgledy-piggledy rooftops to Torre del Mangia and the *duomo*.

Castello delle Serre   BOUTIQUE HOTEL €€€

(☑ 338 5040811; www.castellodelleserre.com; Piazza XX Settembre 1, Serre di Rapolano; d €225-265, ste €275-395; 🅿 ❄ @ 🖥 🖲) The prospect of spending the night in this fabulous medieval castle makes the 40km trip east from Siena well worth the effort. Meticulously restored by the Italian-American Gangale family, it features huge rooms and a swish pool area. For a once-in-a-lifetime experience, book into the deluxe suite in the turret where a private terrace commands suitably regal views.

✕ Eating

Morbidi   DELI €

(www.morbidi.com; Via Banchi di Sopra 75; lunch buffet €12; ⊙ 8am-8pm Mon-Thu, to 9pm Fri & Sat) Possibly the classiest cheap feed in Siena: set in the stylish basement of Morbidi's deli, the lunch buffet on offer here is excellent. For a mere €12, you can join the well-dressed locals sampling antipasti, salads, risottos, pastas and a dessert of the day. Bottled water is supplied, wine and coffee cost extra. Buy your ticket upstairs before heading down.

Grom   GELATERIA €

(www.grom.it; Via Banchi di Sopra 11; gelato €2.50-5.50; ⊙ 11am-midnight summer, to 11pm winter) Delectable gelato with flavours that change with the seasons; many of the ingredients are organic or Slow Food–accredited. They do milkshakes, too.

Enoteca I Terzi   TUSCAN €€

(☑ 0577 4 43 29; www.enotecaiterzi.it; Via dei Termini 7; meals €35-40; ⊙ 11am-1am summer 11am-4pm & 6.30pm-midnight winter, closed Sun) A favourite for many locals who head to this historic *enoteca* (wine bar) to linger over lunches, *aperitivi,* and casual dinners featuring top-notch Tuscan *salumi* (cured meats), delicate handmade pasta and wonderful wines.

Nonna Gina   OSTERIA €€

(☑ 0577 28 72 47; www.osterianonnagina.com; Pian dei Mantellini 2; meals €25-35; ⊙ 12.30-2.30pm & 7.30-10.30pm Tue-Sun) The atmosphere is pure Siena-neighbourhood *osteria*: gingham tablecloths; postcards tacked to the rafters; pictures of Palio jockeys on the walls. The menu speaks of fine local traditions, too: piles of local meat form the *antipasto toscano*, the house red is a very decent Chianti, while the ingredients of the 'secret sauce' covering the plump, cheese-filled gnocchi will never be revealed.

La Compagnia dei Vinattieri   TUSCAN €€
(☑ 0577 23 65 68; www.vinattieri.net; Via delle Terme 79; antipasto platter €7-9, meals €35; ◷ noon-10pm, closed late Feb-late Mar) Duck down the stairs to enjoy a quick glass of wine and a meat or cheese platter in this cellar, or settle in for a leisurely meal; perhaps trying *radicchio* pie with Gorgonzola and walnuts, guinea fowl ravioli, or Tuscan-style cuttlefish stuffed with spinach. To drink? Choose from a 1000-strong wine list.

Tre Cristi   SEAFOOD €€€
(☑ 0577 28 06 08; www.trecristi.com; Vicolo di Provenzano 1; 4-course tasting menus €35-45, 6-course menus €65; ◷ 12.30-2.30pm & 7.30-10pm Mon-Sat) Seafood restaurants are thin on the ground in this meat-obsessed region, so Tre Cristi's long existence (around since 1830) should be heartily celebrated. The menu here is as elegant as the decor, and touches such as a complimentary glass of *prosecco* at the start of the meal add to the experience.

🍷 Drinking

Enoteca Italiana   WINE BAR
(www.enoteca-italiana.it; Fortezza Medicea, Piazza Libertà 1; ◷ noon-midnight Wed-Sat, to 7.30pm Mon & Tue) The former munitions cellar and dun-

geon of this Medici fortress has been artfully transformed into a classy *enoteca* that carries more than 1500 Italian labels. You can take a bottle with you, ship a case home or just enjoy a glass in the attractive courtyard or vaulted interior. There's usually food available, too.

Caffè Fiorella   CAFE
(www.torrefazionefiorella.it; Via di Città 13; ◷ 7am-8pm Mon-Sat) Squeeze into this tiny, heart-of-the-action space to enjoy some of Siena's best coffee. In summer, the coffee *granita* with a dollop of cream is a wonderful indulgence.

Bar Il Palio   CAFE
(Piazza del Campo 47; ◷ 8am-midnight) Arguably the best coffee on the central Campo square; drink it standing at the bar or suffer the financial consequences.

🛍 Shopping

Panificio Il Magnifico   FOOD
(www.ilmagnifico.siena.it; Via dei Pellegrini 27; ◷ 7.30am-7.30pm Mon-Sat) Lorenzo Rossi is Siena's best baker, and his *panforte* (spiced fruit-and-nut cake), *ricciarelli* (sugar-dusted chewy almond biscuits) and *cavallucci* (almond biscuits made with Tuscan honey) are a weekly purchase for most local households. Try them at his bakery and shop behind the *duomo*, and you'll understand why.

Il Pellicano   CERAMICS
(☑ 340 5974038; www.siena-ilpellicano.it; Via Diacceto 17a; ◷ 10.30am-7pm summer, hours vary in winter) Elisabetta Ricci has been making traditional hand-painted Sienese ceramics for over 30 years. She shapes, fires and paints her creations, often using Renaissance-era styles or typical *contrade* designs. Elisabetta also conducts lessons in traditional techniques.

Wednesday Market   MARKET
(◷ 7.30am-1pm) Spreading around Fortezza Medicea and towards the Stadio Comunale, this is one of Tuscany's largest markets and is great for cheap clothing; some food is also sold. An antiques market is held here on the third Sunday of each month.

ⓘ Information

Hospital (☑ 0577 58 51 11; www.ao-siena.toscana.it; Viale Bracci) Just north of Siena at Le Scotte.

Police (☑ 0577 20 11 11; Via del Castoro 6)

Tourist Office (☑ 0577 28 05 51; www.terresiena.it; Piazza del Duomo 1; ◷ 9am-6pm daily summer, 10am-5pm Mon-Sat, to 1pm Sun winter) Provides free Siena city maps, reserves accommodation, organises car and scooter hire, and sells train tickets (commission applies). Also takes bookings for day tours.

ℹ Getting There & Around

CAR & MOTORCYCLE

For Florence, take the RA3 (Siena–Florence *superstrada*) or the more scenic SR222.

There's a Limited Traffic Zone (ZTL) in the historic centre, although visitors can drop off luggage at their hotel, then get out (reception must report your licence number or risk a fine).

Large, conveniently located car parks are at Stadio Comunale and around Fortezza Medicea, both north of Piazza San Domenico. Hotly contested free street parking (look for white lines) is available in Viale Vittorio Veneto, on the southern edge of Fortezza Medicea.

Most car parks charge €2 per hour. For more information see www.sienaparcheggi.com.

Chianti

The ancient vineyards in this part of Tuscany produce the grapes used in Chianti Classico (www.chianticlassico.com), a Sangiovese-dominated drop sold under the Gallo Nero (Black Cockerel) trademark. As well as giving this region its identity, wine also shapes the landscape. The land almost unchanged since ancient times where you'll also encounter historic olive groves, stone farmhouses, dense forests, graceful Romanesque *pievi* (rural churches), Renaissance villas and imposing stone castles built in the Middle Ages by Florentine and Sienese warlords.

Greve in Chianti

POP 14,035

Some 26km south of Florence, Greve is the main town in the Chianti Fiorentino. It's the hub of the local wine industry and has an amiable market-town air, an attractive central square, and tasty eateries and *enoteche*.

Greve's annual wine fair is held in the first or second week of September – book accommodation well in advance.

✕ Eating & Drinking

Mangiando Mangiando TUSCAN €€
(☑ 0558 54 63 72; www.mangiandomangiando.it; Piazza Matteotti 80; meals €30; ☺ noon-3pm & 7-10pm Feb-Dec, closed Thu) When an eatery gives as proud prominence to its list of producers as it does its menu, you know the dishes should be local and good. So it proves in this cheerful, casual eatery, where Tuscan standards

(think rich beef pasta) accompany flavoursome soups, and Chianti Classico (€4.50) and Riserva (€5.50) come by the glass.

Enoteca Falorni WINE BAR
See p48

ℹ Information

Tourist Office (☑ 0558 54 62 99; info@ turismo.greveinchianti.eu; Piazza Matteotti 11; ☺ 10am-7pm summer, reduced hours winter) On Greve's main square.

ℹ Getting There & Around

Find free parking on Piazza della Resistenza. On Fridays, don't park overnight in the paid spaces on Piazza Matteotti – your car will be towed to make room for Saturday market stalls.

Around Greve in Chianti

The vine-etched hills around Greve are idyllic, classic wine-making territory with ample opportunity to explore ancient villages and prestigious wine estates.

◉ Sights & Activities

Antinori nel Chianti Classico WINERY
See p48

Badia a Passignano WINERY
See p48

Castello di Verrazzano WINERY
See p46

🛏 Sleeping

Ostello del Chianti HOSTEL €
(☑ 0558 05 02 65; www.ostellodelchianti.it; Via Roma 137, Tavarnelle Val di Pesa; dm €16, d/q €50/70; ☺ reception 8.30-11am & 4pm-midnight, hostel closed Nov–mid-Mar; P @ 🛜) This is one of Italy's oldest hostels and though it occupies an ugly building in the less-than-scenic town of Tavarnelle Val di Pesa, the friendly staff and bargain prices compensate. Dorms max out at six beds and bike hire can be arranged for €8 per day. Breakfast costs €2. Florence is easily accessed by SITA bus (€3.30, one hour).

Fattoria di Rignana AGRITURISMO €€
(☑ 0558 5 20 65; www.rignana.it; Via di Rignana 15, Rignana; d fattoria €110, without bathroom €95, d villa €140; P @ 🛜 ≋) A chic, historic farmhouse with its very own bell tower rewards you for the drive up the long, rutted road. You'll also find glorious views, a large swimming pool and a very decent eatery. Choose

between elegant rooms in the 17th-century villa and rustic ones in the *fattoria* (farmhouse). It's 4km from Badia a Passignano and 10km west of Greve.

Villa I Barronci HOTEL €€€
(☑0558 2 05 98; www.ibarronci.com; Via Sorripa 10, San Casciano in Val di Pesa; d €190-250; P❋@☎≋⋒) Exemplary service, superb amenities and high comfort levels ensure this modern country hotel is one to remember. You can relax in the bar, rejuvenate in the spa, laze by the pool or head off for easy day trips to Volterra, San Gimignano and Siena. The villa is 20km northwest of Greve, and 15km south of Florence.

🍴 Eating & Drinking

Rinuccio 1180 TUSCAN €€
(☑0552 35 97 20; www.antinorichianticlassico.it; Via Cassia per Siena 133, Bargino; meals €35, tasting platters €10-15; ☺noon-4pm) Imagine lunching inside a glass box on a terrace with an intoxicating 180-degree Dolby-esque surround of hills, birdsong and pea-green vines. This is what the starlet of the Chianti dining scene, set on the uber-high-tech Antinori wine estate in Bargino, is all about. Cuisine is Tuscan, modern, seasonal and sassy. The wine list is (naturally) fabulous. Book ahead.

La Cantinetta di Rignana TUSCAN €€
(☑0558 5 26 01; www.lacantinettadirignana. com; Rignana; meals €40; ☺noon-3pm & 7-10pm Wed-Mon summer, hours vary winter) You might wonder, as you settle onto the terrace here, whether you've found your perfect Chianti lazy lunch location. A historic mill forms the backdrop, vine-lined hills roll off to the horizon and rustic dishes are full of local ingredients and packed with flavour. It's 4km from Badia a Passignano at the end of an unsealed road.

Radda in Chianti & Around

Pretty Radda's age-old streets fan out from its central square, where the shields and escutcheons of the 16th-century **Palazzo del Podestà** add drama to the scene. A historic wine town, it's an appealing base for visits to classic Tuscan vineyards and striking sculpture parks.

⊙ Sights & Activities

Castello di Brolio CASTLE
(☑0577 73 02 80; www.ricasoli.it; garden, chapel & crypt €5, guided tours €8; ☺10am-7pm Apr-Oct,

guided tours every 30min 10.30am-12.30pm & 2.30-5pm Tue-Sun) The ancestral estate of the aristocratic Ricasoli family dates from the 11th century and is the oldest winery in Italy. Currently home to the 32nd baron, it opens its formal garden, panoramic terrace and museum to day-trippers, who often adjourn to the on-site *osteria* for lunch after a guided tour of the castle's small but fascinating museum.

Castello di Ama SCULPTURE
See p49

Parco Sculture del Chianti SCULPTURE
(Chianti Sculpture Park; ☑0577 35 71 51; www. chiantisculpturepark.it; Località La Fornace; adult/child €10/5; ☺10am-dusk Apr-Oct, by appointment Nov-Mar; ⋒) More than 25 site-specific contemporary artworks are tucked into this 13-acre wood, meaning you'll encounter abstract humans, cube clusters and multicoloured cows amid the foliage. Between June and August weekly sunset Jazz and Opera concerts are staged in the park's white Carrara marble and black Zimbabwean granite amphitheatre. Look out for Hitchcock, Fellini and Charlie Chaplin amid the 'spectators'.

🛏 Sleeping

Villa Sassolini BOUTIQUE HOTEL €€€
(☑0559 70 22 46; www.villasassolini.it; Largo Moncioni, Località Moncioni; d €200-345, ste €325-443, dinner €50; ☺closed Nov–mid-Mar; ❋☎≋) It's hard to top the romantic credentials of this gorgeous hotel, set in dense forest on the border of Chianti and the Valdarno. Luxe rooms, an intimate restaurant and a spectacular pool terrace are three of many elements contributing to an utterly irresistible package; proximity to the Valdarno's designer clothing outlet stores being another. It's 25km east of Radda.

🍴 Eating & Drinking

Ristorante La Bottega TUSCAN €€
(☑0577 73 80 01; www.labottegadivolpaia.it; Piazza della Torre 1, Volpaia; meals €25; ☺noon-2.30pm & 7.30-9.30pm Wed-Mon Easter-Jan) *Cucina contadina* (food from the farmers' kitchen) is the mainstay of this pretty restaurant run by the Barucci family – the kitchen garden is right outside and Mum Gina is likely to have made the soup or pasta (her *ribollita* is famous). And what better place to eat it than an outdoor, tree-shaded terrace with sweeping views of Chianti's hills.

Osteria Le Panzanelle   TUSCAN €€

(☑ 0577 73 35 11; www.lepanzanelle.it; Lucarelli; meals €35; ⊙ 12.30-2pm & 7.30-9pm Tue-Sun, closed part of Jan & Feb) An ideal lunch stop en route from Chianti to Siena, this roadside inn serves traditional Tuscan dishes in its garden and downstairs bar-dining room. The menu changes monthly, reflecting what is in season. Find it 5km south of Panzano in Chianti, right next to the SP2 to Radda in Chianti. Bookings are advisable.

Val d'Elsa

A convenient base for visiting the rest of Tuscany, this valley stretching from Chianti to the Maremma regional park ticks many of the boxes on every Tuscan 'must-do' list, with ample opportunity to enjoy fine food, wine, museums and scenery.

San Gimignano

POP 7768

As you crest the nearby hills, the 14 towers of this walled hill town look like a medieval Manhattan. Originally an Etruscan village, the settlement was named after the bishop of Modena, San Gimignano, who is said to have saved the city from Attila the Hun. It became a self-governing *comune* in 1199 and was very prosperous due in part to its location on the Via Francigena – building a tower taller than those built by one's neighbour (there were originally 72) became a popular way for the town's prominent families to flaunt their power and wealth. In 1348 plague wiped out much of the population and weakened the local economy, leading to the town's submission to Florence in 1353.

Today, not even the plague could deter the swarms of summer day trippers, lured here by the town's palpable sense of history, intact medieval streetscapes and enchanting rural setting.

◉ Sights

| **Collegiata** | CHURCH |
| See p22 | |

| **Palazzo Comunale & Torre Grossa** | MUSEUM |
| See p22 | |

| **Pinacoteca** | ART GALLERY |
| See p22 | |

| **Museo del Vino** | MUSEUM |
| See p22 | |

DON'T MISS

GALLERIA CONTINUA

It may seem strange to highlight contemporary art in this medieval time capsule of a town, but there's good reason. **Galleria Continua** (☑ 0577 94 31 34; www.galleriacontinua.com; Via del Castello 11; ⊙ 10am-1pm & 2-7pm Mon-Sat) is one of the best commercial art galleries in Europe, showing the work of big-name artists such as Ai Weiwei, Daniel Buren, Carlos Garaicoa, Moataz Nasr, Kendell Geers and Sophie Whettnall.

Spread over three venues (an old cinema, a medieval tower and a medieval vaulted cellar), the gallery is one of San Gimignano's most compelling attractions.

🛏 Sleeping

Al Pozzo dei Desideri   APARTMENT €

(☑ 370 3102538, 0577 90 71 99; www.alpozzo deidesideri.it; Piazza della Cisterna 32; d/tr/q €110/120/160; ❄🕾) Three rooms-with-a-view (two over the countryside and one over the town's main piazza) are on offer in this gorgeous 13th-century building; expect marble bathrooms, drapes and warm stone walls. All have a fridge and tea- and coffee-making facilities. There's no breakfast, but this is town-centre Tuscany: there's a good cafe close by.

Il Paluffo   AGRITURISMO €€

(☑ 0571 66 42 59; www.paluffo.com; Via Citerna 144, near Lucardo; B&B d €160, 4-/6-person apt per week €1890/2300; ℗❄@🕾🏊) 🍃 Hidden in the hills 20km north of San Gimignano sits the kind of luxurious, innovative, ecological agriturismo that you remember for a very, very long time. At Il Paluffo an inspired conversion of a centuries-old olive farm has seen the former fermentation room transformed into a book-packed, two-story lounge with vast sofas and a kooky feature fireplace.

🍴 Eating & Drinking

San Gimignano is known for its *zafferano* (saffron). You can purchase meat, vegetables, fish and takeaway food at the Thursday morning market in and around the piazzas Cisterna, Duomo and Erbe.

Dal Bertelli   SANDWICHES €

(Via Capassi 30; panini €4-6, glasses of wine €2; ⊙ 1-7pm Mar-early Jan) The Bertelli family has lived

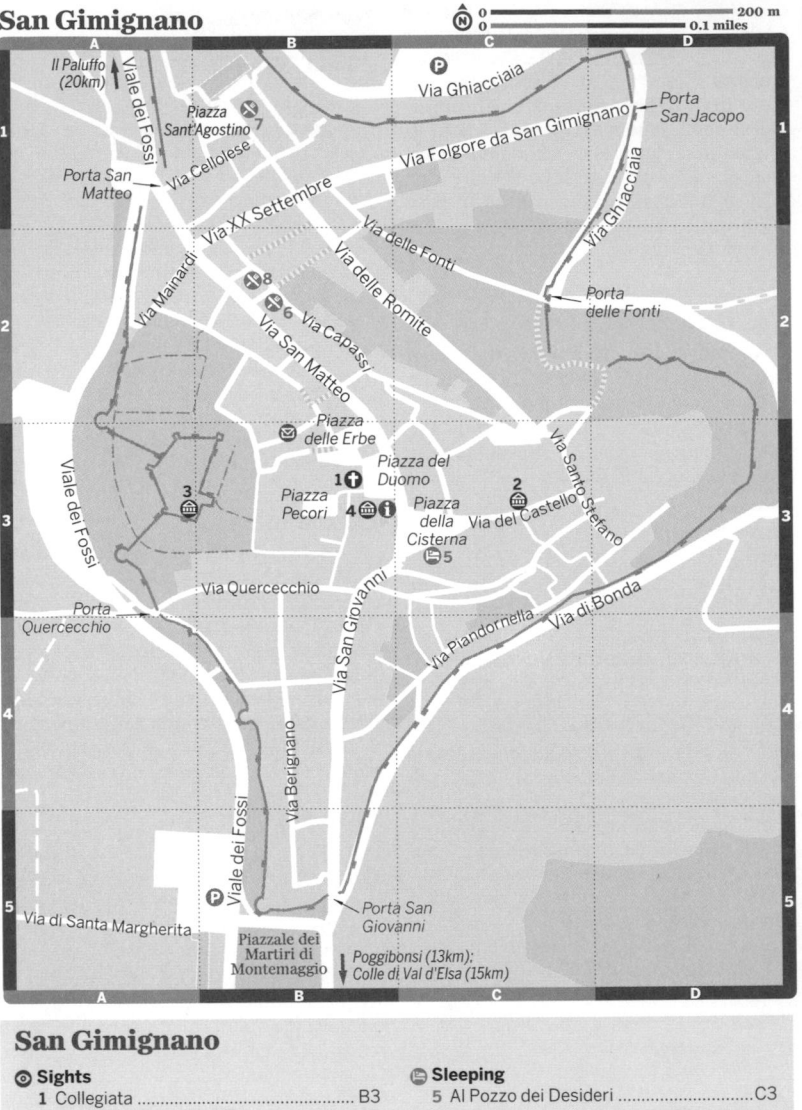

San Gimignano

◎ Sights
1	Collegiata	B3
2	Galleria Continua	C3
3	Museo del Vino	A3
4	Palazzo Comunale & Torre Grossa	B3
	Pinacoteca	(see 4)

🛏 Sleeping
5	Al Pozzo dei Desideri	C3

🍴 Eating
6	Dal Bertelli	B2
7	Locanda Sant'Agostino	B1
8	Perucà	B2

in San Gimignano since 1779, and its current patriarch is fiercely proud of both his heritage and his sandwiches. Salami, cheese, bread and wine is sourced from local artisan pro-

ducers and it's sold in generous portions in a determinedly un-gentrified space with marble surfaces, wooden shelves and curious agricultural implements dangling from stone walls.

Locanda Sant'Agostino TUSCAN €€

(📋 0577 94 31 41; www.locandasantagostino.net; Piazza Sant'Agostino 15; meals €30; ⏰ 12.30-2.30pm & 7-10pm Thu-Tue) It's a bit like eating in an Italian grandmother's kitchen: bundles of dried wheat hang from the ceiling; knick-knacks are stacked on the shelves and the cooking is sublime. Homemade *pici* (thick, hand-rolled pasta) might come with wild-boar *ragù*, while truffles feature strongly – like the servings of Vernaccia wine, they're dished out with an admirably generous hand.

Perucà TUSCAN €€

(📋 0577 94 31 36; www.peruca.eu; Via Capassi 16; meals €30; ⏰ 12.30-2pm & 7.30-10pm Tue-Sun mid-Feb–early Dec, open Mon Apr-Sep) The owner is as knowledgeable about regional food and wine as she is enthusiastic, and the food is excellent. Try the speciality of *fagottini del contadino* (ravioli with *pecorino*, pears and saffron cream) with a glass of Fattoria San Donato's Vernaccia – a match made in heaven.

❶ Information

Tourist Office (📋 0577 94 00 08; www. sangimignano.com; Piazza del Duomo 1; ⏰ 9am-1pm & 3-7pm summer, 9am-1pm & 2-6pm winter) An extremely helpful office which organises tours and supplies maps. It also offers accommodation booking on its website.

❶ Getting There & Away

From Florence and Siena, take the Siena–Florence *superstrada*, then the SR2 and finally the SP1 from Poggibonsi Nord. From Volterra, take the SR68 east and follow the turn-off signs north to San Gimignano on the SP47.

The cheapest parking option (per hour/24 hours €1.50/6) is Parcheggio Giubileo on the southern edge of town; the most convenient is Parcheggio Montemaggio next to Porta San Giovanni (per hour/24 hours €2/20).

Val d'Orcia & Val di Chiana

These two valleys are showcases of classic Tuscan scenery – the landscape of the Val d'Orcia is so magnificent that it is protected as a Unesco World Heritage Site.

Montalcino & Around

This town is defined by the fruit of vines – it's known globally as the home of one of the world's great wines, Brunello di Montalcino. A remarkable number of *enoteche* line its medieval streets.

◉ Sights

Fortezza HISTORIC BUILDING
See p51

Museo Civico e Diocesano d'Arte Sacra MUSEUM
(📋 0577 84 60 14; Via Ricasoli 31; adult/reduced €4.50/3; ⏰ 10am-1pm & 2-5.30pm Tue-Sun) Occupying the former convent of the neighbouring **Chiesa di Sant'Agostino**, this collection of religious art from the town and surrounding region includes a triptych by Duccio and a *Madonna and Child* by Simone Martini. Other artists include the Lorenzetti brothers, Giovanni di Paolo and Sano di Pietro.

Poggio Antico WINERY
(📋 0577 84 80 44; www.poggioantico.com; ⏰ cantina 10am-6pm, restaurant noon-2.30pm & 7-9.30pm Tue-Sun, closed Sun evening winter) Located 5km outside Montalcino on the road to Grosseto, Poggio Antico is a superb foodie one-stop shop. It makes award winning wines (try its Brunello Altero or Riserva), conducts free cellar tours in Italian, English and German, offers paid tastings (approx €25 depending on wines) and has an on-site restaurant (meals €40). Book tours in advance.

🛏 Sleeping

Il Palazzo D&D €
(📋 0577 84 91 10; www.ilpalazzomontalcino.it; Via Panfilo Dell'Oca 23; d €75-80; 🅿 🐾) Il Palazzo manages to both immerse you in aristocratic surroundings and make you feel cosily at home. The rambling 500-year-old building features ornate tile floors, beams, sumptuous tapestries and antique chairs. But it's the friendly welcome and the almost incidental nature of the splendour that really delights. The rates are ridiculously good, too.

Hotel Vecchia Oliviera HOTEL €€
(📋 0577 84 60 28; www.vecchiaoliviera.com; Via Landi 1; s €70-85, d €120-190; 🅿 ❄ 🛜 🏊) With dangling chandeliers, elegant armchairs, polished wooden floors and rich rugs, this converted oil mill has a refined air. The pick of the 11 rooms comes with hill views and a Jacuzzi, the pool is in an attractive garden setting, and the terrace has wrap-around views.

X Eating & Drinking

Il Leccio TUSCAN €€
(☎ 0577 84 41 75; www.illeccio.net; Costa Castellare 1, Sant'Angelo in Colle; meals €40; ☺ noon-3pm & 7-10pm) Sometimes simple dishes are the hardest to perfect, and perfection is the only term to use when discussing this trattoria in Brunello heartland. Watching the chef make his way between his stove and kitchen garden to gather produce for each order puts a whole new spin on the word 'fresh', and both the results and the house Brunello are spectacular.

Osticcio WINE BAR
(www.osticcio.it; Via Matteotti 23; antipasto plates €7-18, meals €37; ☺ noon-4pm & 7-11pm Fri-Wed, plus noon-7pm Thu summer) In a town overflowing with *enoteche*, this is definitely one of the best. A huge selection of Brunello and Rosso di Montalcino accompanies tempting dishes such as marinated anchovies, *cinta senese* (Tuscan pork) crostini, and pasta with pumpkin and pecorino. The panoramic view, meanwhile, almost upstages it all.

Fiaschetteria Italiana 1888 CAFE
(Piazza del Popolo 6; ☺ 7.30am-midnight, closed Thu winter) You could take a seat in the slender square outside this atmosphere-laden *enoteca*-cafe, but then you'd miss its remarkable 19th-century decor – all brass, mirrors and ornate lights. It's been serving coffee and glasses of Brunello to locals since 1888 (hence the name) and is still chock-full of charm.

ⓘ Information

Tourist Office (☎ 0577 84 93 31; www.prolocomontalcino.com; Costa del Municipio 1; ☺ 10am-1pm & 2-5.50pm) The tourist office is just off the main square and can book cellar-door visits and accommodation.

ⓘ Getting There & Away

From Siena, take the SS2 (Via Cassia) after Buonconvento, then turn off onto the SP45. Find parking around the Fortezza (€1.50 per hour).

Pienza

POP 2125

The road to Montepulciano might pass right through Pienza, but that doesn't detract from this pretty town's astonishing appeal. A sleepy hamlet until Enea Silvio Piccolomini (later Pius II) decided to rebuild it in magnificent Renaissance style, Unesco added

Pienza's historic centre to its World Heritage list in 1996, citing the revolutionary vision of urban space realised in Piazza Pio II and the buildings around it.

◉ Sights

Piazza Pio II PIAZZA
See p32

Duomo CATHEDRAL
See p32

Palazzo Piccolomini PALACE
See p32

🛏 Sleeping & Eating

Cavalierino AGRITURISMO €
(☎ 0578 75 87 33; www.cavalierino.it; Via di Poggiano 17; 4-person apt per night/week from €180/1100; P 🔊 🖼) The first thing that strikes you about Cavalierino is the peace. In this hilltop, supremely stylish, organic agriturismo wicker furniture and contemporary paintings blend artfully with bright rooms and terracotta floors. The top-floor bedrooms offer bewitching views of snaking rows of vines; the pool and sauna add to the appeal, as do the washing machines, well-stocked kitchens (including coffee makers) and racks of luxury toiletries. Cavalierino is midway between Pienza and Montepulciano.

La Bandita Townhouse BOUTIQUE HOTEL €€€
(☎ 0578 74 90 05; www.labanditatownhouse.com; Corso Il Rossellino 111; r €250-495; ste €350-695; P ❄ @ 🔊 🖶) There's something irresistible about La Bandita, where 12 dreamily luxurious rooms sit inside a Renaissance-era convent – here age-old stone walls meet sleek leather sofas and suspended beds. But the real joy is the ambition: to give guests a taste of Tuscan village life. Its heart-of-Pienza setting helps, as does a gorgeous communal lounge and a laid-back wine bar.

Osteria Sette di Vino TUSCAN €
(☎ 0578 74 90 92; Piazza di Spagna 1; meals €20; ☺ 12.30-2.30pm & 7.30-10pm Thu-Tue) Known for its *zuppa di pane e fagioli* (bread and white-bean soup), *bruschette* and range of local *pecorino* cheese, this simple place is run by the exuberant Luciano, who is immortalised as Bacchus in a copy of Caravaggio's famous painting hanging above the main counter. There's a clutch of tables inside and a scattering outside – book ahead.

Pummarò PIZZA €

(Via del Giglio 4; slice €2.50, pizza €6-10; ⊗ noon-11pm Tue-Sun; 🛜🍴) Look for brightly painted bicycles in a laneway off Via Rossellino and you'll find this teensy pizzeria, which is a great place to source a cheap and quick snack. There's an innovative range of all-vegetable offerings; the *pizza pummarò* (with cherry tomatoes, buffalo mozzarella and basil) is superb.

❶ Information

Tourist Office (📞 0578 74 99 05; info. turismo@comune.pienza.si.it; Corso Rossellino 30; ⊗ 10am-1pm & 2-5pm Wed-Mon summer, 10am-4pm Sat & Sun winter) Located on the ground floor of Palazzo Borgia.

Monticchiello

Semi-comatose and pretty-as-a-picture, the medieval village of Monticchiello crowns a hill 10km south of Pienza.

🛏️ Sleeping & Eating

La Casa di Adelina B&B €

(📞 0578 75 51 67; www.lacasadiadelina.eu; Piazza San Martino 3; s €55, d €85-105, 4-bed apt €204; @🛜) Laden with art and atmosphere, this place has friendly hosts, a communal lounge with wood stove (a joy in winter) and four delectable, rustic-chic rooms done out in accents of dove-grey and aquamarine. There's also a similarly styled two-bedroom apartment with all the mod-cons that's perfect for an extended stay (discounts available).

Osteria La Porta TUSCAN €€

See p33

Montepulciano

POP 14,290

Exploring this reclaimed narrow ridge of volcanic rock will push your quadriceps to failure point. When this happens, self-medicate with a pour of the highly reputed Vino Nobile while drinking in spectacular views over the Val di Chiana and Val d'Orcia.

◎ Sights

Il Corso STREET

See p52

Palazzo Comunale PALACE

See p52

Montepulciano
DAVID PINZER PHOTOGRAPHY/GETTY IMAGES ©

Museo Civico MUSEUM, ART GALLERY

(www.museocivicomontepulciano.it; Via Ricci 10; adult/reduced €5/3; ⊗ 10am-1pm & 3-6pm Tue-Sun summer, Sat & Sun only winter) Montepulciano's modest museum and pinacoteca have recently had a curatorial dream come true: a painting in their collections has been attributed to Caravaggio. The masterpiece is a characteristic *Portrait of a Gentleman*. Worth the entrance fee alone, it's accompanied by high-tech, touch-screen interpretation, which allows you to explore details of the painting, its restoration and diagnostic attribution.

🛏️ Sleeping

Camere Bellavista HOTEL €

(📞 0578 75 73 48; www.camerebellavista.it; Via Ricci 25; d €75-100; 🅿🛜) As this excellent budget hotel is four stories tall and sits on the edge of the old town, the views live up to its name. The styling is heritage rustic with exposed beams, hefty wooden furniture, brass bedsteads and smart new bathrooms. The owner isn't resident, so phone ahead to be met with the key. No breakfast.

Locanda San Francesco B&B €€

(📞 0578 75 87 25; www.locandasanfrancesco.it; Piazza San Francesco 3; d €160-250; 🅿❄@🛜) There's only one downside to this B&B: once you check into this supremely welcoming, 14th century *palazzo*, you might never want to go. The feel is elegant but also homely:

PARCO REGIONALE DELLA MAREMMA

This spectacular **regional park** (www.parco-maremma.it; park admission adult/reduced €10/5) incorporates the Uccellina mountain range, a 600-hectare pine forest, marshy plains and a 20km stretch of unspoiled coastline. The main **visitor centre** (☑0564 40 70 98; Via del Bersagliere 7-9, Alberese; ☉8am-6pm mid-Jun–mid-Sep, to 4pm mid-Sep–mid-Nov, to 2pm mid-Nov–mid-Jun) is in Alberese, on the park's northern edge.

Park access is limited to 13 signed walking trails, varying in length from 2.5km to 13km; the most popular is A2 ('Le Torri'), a 5.8km walk to the beach. The entry fee (paid at the visitor centre) varies according to whether a park-operated bus transports you from the visitor centre to your chosen route. From 15 June to 15 September the park can only be visited on a guided tour due to possible bushfire threat.

As well as the walking trails, there are four guided mountain-bike tours (€20 to €25, two to six hours) and a guided 2½-hour canoe tour (adult/child €16/10); book these at the visitor centre. Private operators run horse and pony treks in the park – contact **Il Gelsomino** (☑0564 40 5 133; www.ilgelsomino.com; Via Strada del Barbicato 4, Alberese; treks from €30) or **Circolo Ippico Uccellina** (☑334 9797181; www.circoloippicouccellina.it; Località Collecchio 38, Magliano in Toscana; per half-/full day from €55/95).

refined furnishings meet well-stocked bookshelves; restrained fabrics are teamed with fluffy bathrobes. The best room has superb views over the Val d'Orcia on one side and the Val di Chiana on the other.

Fattoria San Martino AGRITURISMO €€
(☑0578 71 74 63; www.fattoriasanmartino.it; Via di Martiena 3; r €140-180; ☉closed Dec-Easter; P☎❄❀) ✐ Dutch-born Karin and Italian Antonio met when working in Milan's high-velocity fashion industry, but eventually decided organic farming was more to their liking than haute couture. The homespun-chic rooms in this rebuilt 12th-century farmhouse and purpose-built annexe are sure to please, as will the all-vegetarian meals (dinner €35 plus wine), pretty garden, biological filtered pool and emphasis on sustainability.

✕ Eating & Drinking

Osteria Acquacheta TUSCAN €€
(☑0578 71 70 86; www.acquacheta.eu; Via del Teatro 2; meals €25; ☉12.15-4pm & 7.30-10.30pm Wed-Mon) Hugely popular with locals and tourists alike, this bustling *osteria* specialises in *bistecca alla fiorentina* (chargrilled T-bone steak), which arrives in huge, lightly seared, exceptionally flavoursome slabs (don't even *think* of asking for it to be served otherwise). Lunch sittings are at 12.15pm and 2.15pm; dinner at 7.30pm and 9.15pm – book ahead.

La Grotta RISTORANTE €€€
(☑0578 75 74 79; www.lagrottamontepulciano. it; Via San Biagio 15; meals €44, 6-course tasting menu €48; ☉12.30-2.30pm & 7.30-10pm Thu-Tue, closed mid-Jan–mid-Mar) The ingredients, and sometimes dishes, may be traditional, but the presentation is full of refined flourishes – artfully arranged Parmesan shavings and sprigs of herbs crown delicate towers of pasta, vegetables and meat. The service is exemplary and the courtyard garden divine. It's just outside town on the road to Chiusi.

ℹ Information

Tourist Office (☑0578 75 73 41; www.proloco montepulciano.it; Piazza Don Minzoni 1; ☉9.30am-12.30pm & 3-6pm Mon-Sat, 9.30am-12.30pm Sun) Reserves last-minute accommodation (in person only), offers internet access (€3.50 per hour), supplies town maps, can advise on mountain bike and scooter rental (€25 to €50) and sells bus and train tickets (€1 commission applies for train tickets).

SOUTHERN TUSCANY

With its landscape of dramatic coastlines, mysterious Etruscan sites and medieval hilltop villages, this little-visited pocket of Tuscany offers contrasts galore. It's a region created for the Italy connoisseur.

Città del Tufa

Sovana

POP 100

Built by the Romans, this postcard-pretty village with a cobbled main street hides away two austerely beautiful Romanesque churches, a museum showcasing a collection of ancient gold coins and Etruscan treasures.

⊙ Sights

**Parco Archeologico della Città
del Tufa**   ARCHAEOLOGICAL SITE
See p38

Duomo   CATHEDRAL
See p38

Santa Maria Maggiore   CHURCH
See p38

🛏 Sleeping & Eating

Taverna Etrusca   HOTEL €
(☑ 0564 61 41 13; www.tavernaetrusca.com; Piazza del Pretorio 16; d €80-90, meals €20-60; 🐾) Sovana's rich heritage can certainly be felt in these stylish lodgings. Twisting wooden stairs lead to stately rooms made atmospheric by artful lighting and stone walls. Downstairs, refined modern Tuscan cuisine is served in a shaded courtyard garden and brick-and-beam dining room. The 30-page *carta dei vini* (wine list) features both Sovana and Morellino di Scansano DOC wines.

Pitigliano

POP 3878

Check your car mirrors before screeching to a halt and indulging in an orgy of photography on the approach to this spectacular hilltop stronghold, surrounded by gorges on three sides to create a natural bastion completed by a constructed fortress. Within the Old Town, twisting stairways disappear around corners, cobbled alleys bend tantalisingly out of sight beneath graceful arches and stone houses are crammed next to each other in a higgledy-piggledy fashion.

⊙ Sights & Activities

There's a fine walk from Pitigliano to Sovana (8km) that incorporates parts of the *vie cave* (sunken roads) hewn out of tufa in the valleys below Pitigliano. The enormous passages – up to 20m deep and 3m wide – are believed to be sacred routes linking Etruscan necropolises and other religious sites. For a description and map, go to www.trekking.it and download the pdf in the Maremma section.

La Piccola Gerusalemme   MUSEUM
See p40

**Museo Civico Archeologico
della Civiltà Etrusca**   MUSEUM
See p40

🛏 Sleeping & Eating

Le Camere del Ceccottino   PENSION €€
(☑ 0564 61 42 73; www.ceccottino.com; Via Roma 159; r €80-150; ✳🐾) Owned and operated by the extremely helpful Chiara and Alessandro, who also run a nearby *osteria* and *enoteca* of the same name, this *pensione* boasts an excellent location near the *duomo* and four immaculately maintained and well-equipped rooms. Opt for the superior or prestige room if possible, as the standard versions are a little small. No breakfast.

La Rocca   TUSCAN, WINE BAR €
(Piazza della Repubblica 92; panino €4, meals €28; ⊙10am-3am Tue-Sat, to midnight Sun) Generous pourings of local wine, including Pitigliano's very own DOC white, are on offer at this cavernous wine bar, tucked away at the far end of Piazza della Repubblica, near the panoramic viewpoint. The range of *prodotti tipici* (typical local products) is impressive – choose from rustic pastas, antipasti platters and *panini* stuffed with cured meats and *pecorino* cheese.

Il Tufo Allegro   TUSCAN €€
(☑ 0564 61 61 92; www.iltufoallegro.com; Vicolo della Costituzione 5; meals €22-70; ⊙noon-1.30pm Thu-Mon & 7.30-9.30pm Wed-Mon Mar-Dec) The aromas emanating from the kitchen door off Via Zuccarelli should be enough to draw you down the stairs and into the cosy dining rooms, which are carved out of tufa. Chef Domenico Pichini's menus range from traditional to modern, and all of his creations rely heavily on local produce for inspiration. It's near La Piccola Gerusalemme museum.

❶ Information

Tourist Office (☑ 0564 61 71 11; www.comune.pitigliano.gr.it; Piazza Garibaldi 12; ⊙10am-12.30pm & 3.30-6pm Tue-Sat summer, 10am-12.30pm & 3-5.30pm Fri & Sat, 10am-12.30pm Sun winter) In the piazza just inside the Old City's main gate.

Pisa & Northern Tuscany

There is more to this green corner of Tuscany than the Leaning Tower. Linger over regional specialities, and meander along ancient pilgrim routes. Even the largest towns – university hub Pisa and 'love at first sight' Lucca – have an air of tranquillity and tradition. This is snail-paced Italy, impossible not to love.

PISA

POP 88,627

Once a maritime power to rival Genoa and Venice, Pisa now draws its fame from an architectural project gone terribly wrong. But the world-famous Leaning Tower is just one of many noteworthy sights in this compact and compelling city. Education has fuelled the local economy since the 1400s, and students from across Italy still compete for places in its elite university and research schools. This endows the centre of town with a vibrant and affordable cafe and bar scene, and balances an enviable portfolio of well-maintained Romanesque buildings, Gothic churches and Renaissance piazzas with a lively street life dominated by locals rather than tourists.

◉ Sights

Many visitors to Pisa arrive by train at Stazione San Rossore and don't get any further than neighbouring Piazza dei Miracoli. Those in the know arrive or depart using Pisa's Stazione Centrale allowing casual discovery of the *centro storico* (historic centre).

Piazza dei Miracoli SQUARE
No Tuscan sight is more immortalised in kitsch souvenirs than the iconic tower teetering on the edge of this gargantuan piazza, which is called both the Campo dei Miracoli (Field of Miracles) and Piazza del Duomo (Cathedral Sq). The piazza's expansive green lawns provide an urban carpet on which Europe's most extraordinary concentration of Romanesque buildings – in the form of the cathedral, baptistry and tower – are arranged. With two million visitors every year, crowds are the norm, many arriving by tour bus from Florence for a whirlwind visit.

Leaning Tower TOWER
(Torre Pendente; www.opapisa.it; Piazza dei Miracoli; admission €18; ☉ 9am-8pm summer, 10am-5pm winter) One of Italy's signature sights, the Torre Pendente truly lives up to its name, leaning a startling 3.9 degrees off the vertical. The 56m-high tower, officially the Duomo's *campanile* (bell tower), took almost 200 years to build, but was already listing when it was unveiled in 1372. Over time, the tilt, caused by a layer of weak subsoil, steadily worsened until it was finally halted by a major stabilisation project in the 1990s.

Duomo CATHEDRAL
(www.opapisa.it; Piazza dei Miracoli; ☉ 10am-8pm summer, 10am-12.45pm & 2-5pm winter) FREE Pisa's magnificent Romanesque Duomo was begun in 1064 and consecrated in 1118. Its striking tiered exterior, with cladding of green-and-cream marble bands, gives on to a vast col-

umned interior capped by a gold wooden ceiling. The elliptical dome, the first of its kind in Europe at the time, was added in 1380.

Note that while admission is free, you'll need an entrance coupon from the ticket office or a ticket from one of the other Piazza dei Miracoli sights.

Battistero RELIGIOUS SITE
(Baptistry; www.opapisa.it; Piazza dei Miracoli; adult/reduced €5/3, combination ticket with Camposanto & Museo delle Sinópie 2/3 sights €7/8 (reduced €4/5); ⊙8am-8pm summer, 10am-5pm Nov-Feb) Pisa's unusual round baptistry has one dome piled on top of another, each roofed half in lead, half in tiles, and topped by a gilt-bronze John the Baptist (1395). Construction began in 1152, but it was remodelled and continued by Nicola and Giovanni Pisano more than a century later and finally completed in the 14th century. Inside, the hexagonal marble pulpit (1260) by Nicola Pisano is the highlight.

⊙ Along the Arno

Away from the crowded heavyweights of Piazza dei Miracoli, along the Arno river banks, Pisa comes into its own. Splendid *palazzi* (mansions), painted a multitude of hues, line the southern *lungarno* (riverside embankment), from where shopping boulevard Corso Italia legs it to the central train station, Stazione Centrale.

Pisa's medieval heart lies north of the water: from riverside **Piazza Cairoli**, with its bars and gelaterie, meander along Via Cavour and lose yourself in ancient backstreets. A daily fresh-produce market fills **Piazza delle Vettovaglie**, ringed with 15th-century porticoes and cafe terraces.

WESTEND61/GETTY IMAGES ©

Duomo and Leaning Tower, Piazza dei Miracoli

Pisa

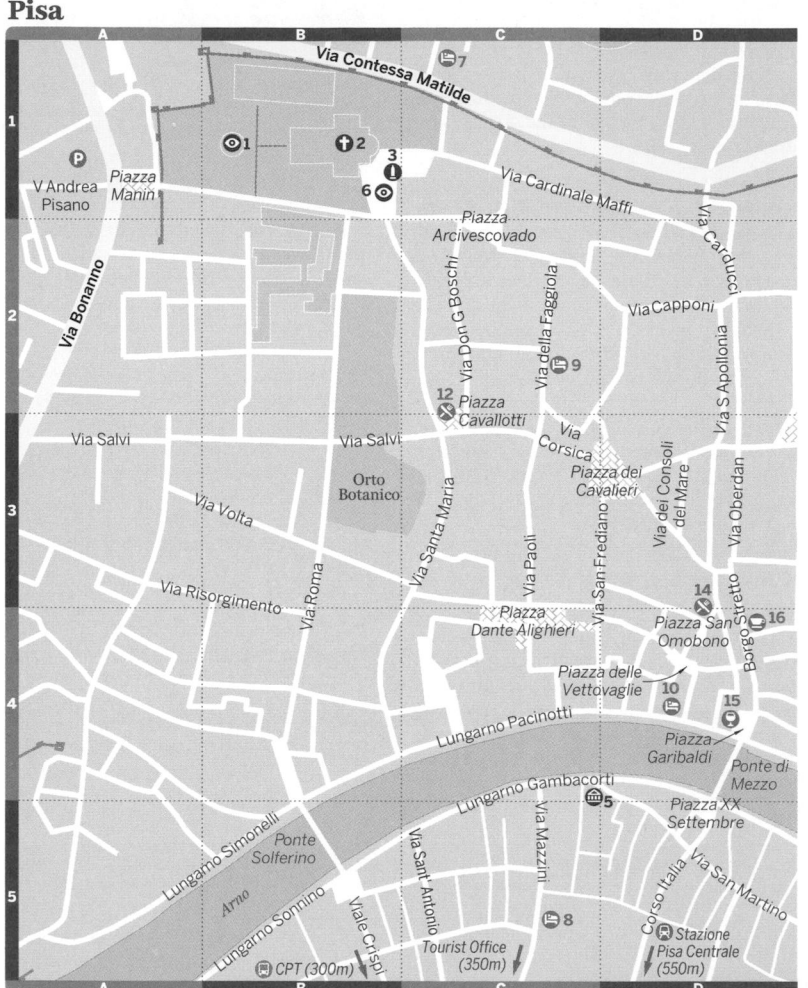

Palazzo Blu   GALLERY
(www.palazzoblu.it; Lungarno Gambacorti 9; ⏰10am-7pm Tue-Fri, to 8pm Sat & Sun) **FREE** Facing the river is this magnificently restored, 14th-century building that has a striking dusty-blue facade. Inside, its over-the-top 19th-century interior decoration is the perfect backdrop for the Foundation Pisa's art collection – predominantly Pisan works from the 14th to the 20th centuries, plus various temporary exhibitions.

Museo Nazionale di San Matteo   MUSEUM
(Piazza San Matteo in Soarta; adult/reduced €5/2.50; ⏰8.30am-7.30pm Tue-Sat, to 1.30pm Sun) This repository of medieval masterpieces sits in a 13th-century Benedictine convent on the Arno's northern waterfront boulevard. The museum's collection of paintings from the Tuscan school is notable, with works by Lippo Memmi, Taddeo Gaddi, Gentile da Fabriano and Ghirlandaio. Don't miss Masaccio's *St Paul*, Fra' Angelico's *Madonna of Humility* and Simone Martini's *Polyptych of Saint Catherine*.

Pisa

◎ Sights
1	Battistero	B1
2	Duomo	B1
3	Leaning Tower	B1
4	Museo Nazionale di San Matteo	F5
5	Palazzo Blu	C4
6	Piazza dei Miracoli	B1

🛌 Sleeping
7	Hostel Pisa Tower	C1
8	Hotel Bologna	C5
9	Hotel Relais dell'Orologio	C2
10	Royal Victoria Hotel	D4

✖ Eating
11	biOsteria 050	E3
12	L'Ostellino	C2
13	Osteria Bernardo	E4
14	Pizzeria Il Montino	D3

🍸 Drinking & Nightlife
15	Bazeel	D4
16	Salza	D4
17	Sottobosco	E4

⭐ Festivals & Events

Luminaria di San Ranieri LIGHT SHOW

(⏱16 Jun) The night before Pisa's patron saint's day is magical: thousands upon thousands of candles and blazing torches light up the river and riverbanks while fireworks bedazzle the night sky.

Regata Storica di San Ranieri SPORTS

(⏱17 Jun) The Arno comes to life with a rowing regatta to commemorate the city's patron saint.

Gioco del Ponte CULTURAL

(⏱Jun) During Gioco del Ponte (Game of the Bridge), two teams in medieval costume battle it out over the Ponte di Mezzo; last Sunday in June.

🛏 Sleeping

Hostel Pisa Tower HOSTEL €

(☏050 520 24 54; www.hostelpisatower.it; Via Piave 4; dm €20-25; @🛜) This super-friendly hostel occupies a suburban villa a couple of minutes' walk from Piazza dei Miracoli. It's bright and cheery, with colourful decor, female and mixed dorms, communal kitchen, and a summer-friendly terrace overlooking a small grassy garden. Dorms are named, meaning you can sleep with Galileo, Mona Lisa, Leonardo or Michelangelo.

Royal Victoria Hotel HOTEL €€

(☏050 94 01 11; www.royalvictoria.it; Lungarno Pacinotti 12; d €95-170, tr €105-180; ❄🛜🚙) This doyen of Pisan hotels, run by the Piegaja family since 1837, offers old-world luxury accompanied by warm, attentive service. Its 38 rooms exude a shabby-chic spirit with their Grand Tour antiques, although renovations are imminent. Don't miss an *aperitivo* flopped on a sofa on the 4th-floor terrace, packed with potted plants. Garage parking/bike hire €20/15 per day, breakfast €5.

Hotel Bologna
HOTEL €€

(☎050 50 21 20; www.hotelbologna.pisa.it; Via Giuseppe Mazzini 57; d/tr €148/188; P✳🖙📶) Placed well away from the Piazza dei Miracoli mayhem, this elegant four-star mansion hotel is an oasis of peace and tranquillity. Its big, bright rooms have wooden floors and colour-coordinated furnishings – some are frescoed. Kudos for the small terrace and cypress-shaded garden out the back – delightful for lazy summertime breakfasts. Reception organises bike/scooter hire; courtyard parking for motorists €12 per night.

Hotel Relais dell'Orologio
HOTEL €€€

(☎050 83 03 61; www.hotelrelaisorologio.com; Via della Faggiola 12-14; d €150-240; ✳📶) Something of a honeymoon venue, Pisa's dreamy five-star hotel occupies a tastefully restored 14th-century fortified tower housed in a quiet backstreet. Some rooms have original frescoes and the flowery patio restaurant is a welcome retreat from the crowds. Book online to bag the cheapest deal – non-refundable, early-booking rates are best value.

✗ Eating

L'Ostellino
SANDWICHES €

(Piazza Felice Cavallotti 1; panini €3-6; ⊗11.30am-4.30pm Mon-Fri, to 6pm Sat & Sun) For a buster-size gourmet *panino* (sandwich) wrapped in crunchy waxed paper, this miniscule deli and *pannineria* (sandwich shop) with just a handful of tables delivers. Take your pick from dozens of different combos written by hand on the blackboard (*lardo di colonnata* with figs or cave-aged *pecorino* with honey and walnuts are sweet favourites), await

construction, then hit the green lawns of Piazza dei Miracoli to picnic with the crowds.

Pizzeria Il Montino
PIZZA €

(☎050 59 86 95; www.pizzeriailmontino.com; Vicolo del Monte 1; pizzas €6-8, foccacine €2.50-4; ⊗10.30am-3pm & 5-10pm Mon-Sat) There is nothing flash or fancy about this down-to-earth pizzeria, an icon among Pisans, student or sophisticate alike. Take away or order at the bar then grab a table, inside or out, and munch on house specialities such as *cecina* (chickpea pizza), *castagnaccio* (chestnut cake) and *spuma* (sweet, nonalcoholic drink). Or go for a *focaccine* (small flat roll) filled with salami, pancetta or *porchetta* (suckling pig).

Hidden in a back alley, the quickest way to find Il Montino is to head west along Via Ulisse Dini from the northern end of Borgo Stretto (opposite the Lo Sfizio cafe at Borgo Stretto 54) to Piazza San Felice where it is easy to spot, on your left, a telling blue neon 'Pizzeria' sign.

Osteria Bernardo
TUSCAN €€

(☎050 57 52 16; www.osteriabernardo.it; Piazza San Paolo all'Orto 1; meals €35; ⊗8-11pm Tue-Sat, 12.30-2.30pm & 8-11pm Sun) This small bistro on one of Pisa's loveliest squares, well away from the madding Leaning Tower crowd, is the perfect fusion of easy dining and gourmet excellence. Its menu is small – just four or five dishes to choose from for each course – and cuisine is creative. The wild-boar *pappardelle* (wide flat pasta strips) scented with chocolate is a great change from the norm.

---

❶ HOW TO FALL IN LOVE WITH PISA

Sure, the iconic Leaning Tower is the reason everyone wants to go to Pisa. But once you've put yourself through the Piazza dei Miracoli madness (littered lawns, football-playing school groups, photo-posing pandemonium...), there's a good chance you'll simply want to get out of town.

To avoid leaving Pisa feeling oddly deflated by one of Europe's great landmarks, save the Leaning Tower and its oversized square for the latter part of the day – or, better still, an enchanting visit after dark (mid-June to August) when the night casts a certain magic on the glistening white monuments and the tour buses have long gone.

Upon arrival, indulge instead in peaceful meanderings along the Arno river, over its bridges and through Pisa's medieval heart. Discover the last monumental wall painting Keith Haring (www.keithcafe.com; Via Zandonai 4; ⊗7am-11pm; 📶) did before he died; enjoy low-key architectural and artistic genius at the riverside Palazzo Blu (p90) and Pisan-Gothic Chiesa di Santa Maria della Spina on Lungarno Gambacorti (built between 1230 and 1223 to house a reliquary of a thorn from Christ's crown); and lunch with locals at Sottobosco (p93).

And only once you've fallen in love with the other Pisa, head for the tower.

biOsteria 050

VEGETARIAN **€€**

(📞 050 54 31 06; www.biosteria050.it; Via San Francesco 36; meals €25-30; ⏰12.30-2.30pm & 7.30-10.30pm Tue-Sat, 7.30-10.30pm Mon & Sun; 🖉) 🖉 Everything that Marco and Raffaele at Zero Cinquanta cook up is strictly seasonal, local and organic, with products from farms within a 50km radius of Pisa. Feast on dishes like risotto with almonds and asparagus, or go for one of the excellent-value lunch specials.

🍷 Drinking

Most drinking action takes place on and around Piazza delle Vettovaglie and the university on cafe-ringed Piazza Dante Alighieri, always packed with students.

Sottobosco

CAFE

(www.sottoboscocafe.it; Piazza San Paolo all'Orto; ⏰10am-midnight Tue-Fri, noon-1am Sat, 7pm-midnight Sun) This creative cafe with books for sale and funky furnishings induces love at first sight. Tuck into a doughnut and cappuccino at a glass-topped table filled with artists' crayons perhaps, or a collection of buttons. Lunch dishes (salads, pies and pasta) are simple and homemade, and come dusk, jazz bands play or DJs spin tunes.

Bazeel

BAR

(www.bazeel.it; Lungarno Pacinotti 1; ⏰7.30am-2am) A dedicated all-rounder, Bazeel is a hot spot from dawn to dark. Laze over breakfast, save cents with a great-value buffet lunch (two/three courses €8/10) or hang out with the A crowd over a generous *aperitivo* spread, live music and DJs. Its chapel-like interior is nothing short of fabulous, as is its pavement terrace out front. Check its Twitter feed @bazeelpisa for what's on.

Salza

CAFE

(Borgo Stretto 44; ⏰8.15am-8pm Tue-Sun) This old-fashioned cake shop has been tempting Pisans into sugar-induced wickedness since 1898. It's an equally lovely spot for a cocktail – anytime.

ℹ Information

Tourist Office (📞 050 4 22 91; www.pisaunicaterra.it; Piazza Vittorio Emanuele II 16; ⏰10am-1pm & 2-4pm)

ℹ Getting There & Around

AIR

Pisa International Airport (Galileo Galilei Airport; 📞 050 84 93 00; www.pisa-airport. com) Tuscany's main international airport, a

Piazza Anfiteatro (p94), Lucca
HANS-PETER MERTEN/GETTY IMAGES ©

10-minute drive south of Pisa; flights to most major European cities.

TO/FROM THE AIRPORT

Train

PisaMover Buses link the airport with Pisa Centrale train station (€1.80, eight minutes, every 10 minutes). From December 2015 this shuttle-bus service will be replaced by a super-speedy, fully automated rail link also called PisaMover; check the Pisa airport website for details.

Bus

The LAM Rossa (red) bus line (€1.10, 10 minutes, every 10 to 20 minutes) passes through the city centre and the train station en route to/from the airport. Buy tickets from the blue ticket machine, next to the bus stops to the right of the train station exit.

Taxi

A taxi between the airport and city centre costs around €10. To book, call **Radio Taxi Pisa** (📞 050 54 16 00; www.cotapi.it).

CAR

Pisa is close to the A11 and A12. The SCG FI-PI-LI (SS67) is a toll-free alternative for Florence and Livorno, while the north–south SS1, the Via Aurelia, connects the city with La Spezia and Rome.

Parking costs up to €2 per hour; don't park in the historic centre's Limited Traffic Zone (ZTL). There's a free car park outside the zone on Lungarno Guadalongo near the Fortezza di San Gallo on the south side of the Arno.

Lucca

POP 86,204

Lovely Lucca endears itself to everyone who visits. Hidden behind imposing Renaissance walls, its cobbled streets, handsome piazzas and shady promenades make it a perfect destination to explore by foot – as a day trip from Florence or in its own right. At the day's end, historic cafes and restaurants tempt visitors to relax over a glass or two of Lucchesi wine and a slow progression of rustic dishes prepared with fresh produce from nearby Garfagnana.

Founded by the Etruscans, Lucca became a Roman colony in 180 BC and a free *comune* (self-governing city) during the 12th century, when it enjoyed a period of prosperity based on the silk trade. In 1314 it briefly fell under the control of Pisa but under the leadership of local adventurer Castruccio Castracani degli Antelminelli, the city regained its freedom, to remain an independent republic for almost 500 years.

◎ Sights

Stone-paved Via Fillungo, with its fashion boutiques and car-free mantra, threads its way through the medieval heart of the old city. East is one of Tuscany's loveliest piazzas, oval cafe-ringed **Piazza Anfiteatro**, named after the amphitheatre that was here in Roman times. Spot remnants of the amphitheatre's brick arches and masonry on the exterior walls of the medieval houses ringing the piazza.

City Wall   HISTORIC SITE
Lucca's monumental *mura* (wall) was built around the old city in the 16th and 17th centuries and remains in almost perfect condition. It superceded two previous walls, the first built from travertine stone blocks as early as the 2nd century BC. Twelve metres high and 4.2km long, today's ramparts are crowned with a tree-lined footpath looking down on the *centro storico* and out towards the Apuane Alps. This path is a favourite location for the locals' daily *passeggiata* (traditional evening stroll).

Cattedrale di San Martino   CATHEDRAL
(www.museocattedralelucca.it; Piazza San Martino; adult/reduced €3/2, with museum & Chiesa e Battistero dei SS Giovanni & Reparata €7/5; ◎9.30am-5pm Mon-Fri, to 6pm Sat, 11.30am-5pm Sun) Lucca's predominantly Romanesque cathedral dates to the 11th century. Its stunning facade was constructed in the prevailing Lucca-Pisan

style and designed to accommodate the pre-existing *campanile* (bell tower). The reliefs over the left doorway of the portico are believed to be by Nicola Pisano, while inside, treasures include the **Volto Santo** (literally, Holy Countenance) crucifix sculpture and a wonderful 15th-century tomb in the sacristy. The cathedral interior was rebuilt in the 14th and 15th centuries with a Gothic flourish.

Museo della Cattedrale   MUSEUM
(www.museocattedralelucca.it; Piazza San Martino; adult/reduced €4/3, with cathedral sacristy & Chiesa e Battistero dei SS Giovanni & Reparata €7/5; ◎10am-6pm) The cathedral museum safeguards elaborate gold and silver decorations made for the Volto Santo, including a 17th-century crown and a 19th-century sceptre.

Torre Guinigi   TOWER
(Via Guinigi; adult/reduced €4/3; ◎9.30am-6.30pm summer, 10.30am-4.30pm winter) The bird's-eye view from the top of this medieval, 45m-tall red-brick tower adjoining 14th-century **Palazzo Guinigi** is predictably magnificent. But what impresses even more are the seven oak trees planted in a U-shaped flower bed at the top of the tower. Legend has it that upon the death of powerful Lucchese ruler Paolo Guinigi (1372–1432) all the leaves fell off the trees. Count 230 steps to the top.

✦ Festivals & Events

Lucca Summer Festival   MUSIC
(www.summer-festival.com; ◎Jul) This month-long festival brings rock and pop stars to Lucca.

⌑ Sleeping

Piccolo Hotel Puccini   HOTEL €
(☏0583 5 54 21; www.hotelpuccini.com; Via di Poggio 9; s/d €75/100; ❄🛜) In a brilliant central location, this welcoming three-star hotel hides behind a discreet brick exterior. Its small guest rooms are attractive with wooden floors, vintage ceiling fans and colourful, contemporary design touches. Breakfast, optional at €3.50, is served at candlelit tables behind the small reception area. Rates are around 30% lower in winter.

Locanda Vigna Ilaria   B&B €€
(☏0583 33 20 91; www.locandavignailaria.it; Via della Pieve Santo Stefano 967c, St Alessio; d/q €110/120; 🅿) Tuscan roadtrippers will be smitten with this stone house in a wealthy surburb, 4km north of Lucca's walled city

Lucca

in St Alessio (dump the car, then meander along green lanes, past vast villas bathed in olive groves). The *locanda* (inn) has five rooms furnished with a mix of old, new and upcycled – lots of wine boxes!

Alla Corte degli Angeli BOUTIQUE HOTEL €€€
(☏ 0583 46 92 04; www.allacortedegliangeli. com; Via degli Angeli 23; s/d/ste €150/250/400; ❄ @ 🛜) This boutique hotel sits in a couple of 15th-century townhouses, with stylish beamed lounge leading to 21 sunny rooms adorned with frescoed ceilings, patches of exposed brick and landscape murals. Every room is named after a different flower, and up-to-the-minute bathrooms have Jacuzzi tubs and power-jet showers. Breakfast €10.

 **Eating**

Da Felice PIZZA €
(www.pizzeriadafelice.it; Via Buia 12; focaccias €1-3, pizza slices €1.30; ⏱ 11am-8.30pm Mon, 10am-

Lucca

◉ Sights

8.30pm Tue-Sat) This buzzing spot behind Piazza San Michele is where the locals come for wood-fired pizza, *cecina* and *castagnacci*. Eat in or take away, each *castagnaccio* comes wrapped in crisp paper, and my, it's good married with a chilled bottle of Moretti beer.

Carnevale, Viareggio

Ristorante Giglio TUSCAN €€
(⌨ 0583 49 40 58; www.ristorantegiglio.com; Piazza del Giglio 2; meals €35; ⊘12.30-2pm & 7.30-10pm Thu-Mon, 7.30-10pm Wed) Don't let the tacky plastic-covered pavement terrace deter you. Splendidly at home in the frescoed 18th-century Palazzo Arnolfini, Giglio is stunning. Dine at white-tableclothed tables, sip a complimentary *prosecco,* watch the fire crackle in the marble fireplace and savour traditional Tuscan with a modern twist: think fresh artichoke salad served in an edible parmesan-cheese wafer 'bowl', or risotto simmered in Chianti.

Local Food Market DELI €€
(⌨ 0583 31 10 77; Via San Paolino 116; meals €30; ⊘10am-11.30pm Tue-Sun) This bright modern address is hidden in a courtyard, complete with potted lemon plants and tables in the sun. In keeping with the seemingly latest trend sweeping through Tuscany, Local Food Market is just that – an upmarket food market, deli and health food shop where you can eat between shelves stacked high with local Tuscan products.

ⓘ Information

Tourist Office (⌨ 0583 58 31 50; www.lucca itinera.it; Piazzale Verdi; ⊘9am-7pm summer, to 5pm winter) Free hotel reservations, left-luggage service (two bags €2.50/4.50/7 per hour/half-day/day) and guided city tours in English departing daily at 2pm (€10, two hours).

ⓘ Getting There & Away

CAR & MOTORCYCLE
The A11 runs westwards to Pisa and Viareggio and eastwards to Florence. The easiest parking is Parcheggio Carducci, just outside Porta Sant'Anna. Within the walls, most car parks are for residents only, indicated by yellow lines. Blue lines indicate where anyone can park (€2 per hour).

ⓘ Getting Around

Rent wheels (ID required) to pedal the 4.2km circumference of Lucca's romantic city walls from a couple of outlets on Piazza Santa Maria, or try the following:

Tourist Center Lucca (⌨ 0583 49 44 01; www. touristcenterlucca.com; Piazzale Ricasoli 203; bike per hour/3hr/day €4/8/12; ⊘8.30am-7.30pm summer, 9am-6pm winter) Exit the train station and bear left to find this handy bike rental outlet, with kids' bikes, tandems, trailers and various other gadgets. It also has left-luggage facilities.

Pietrasanta

POP 24,237
Often overlooked by Tuscan travellers, this refined art town is an unexpected and beautiful surprise. Its bijou historic heart, originally walled, is car-free and loaded with tiny art galleries, workshops and fashion boutiques – perfect for a day's amble broken only by lunch.

Founded in 1255 by Guiscardo da Pietrasanta, *podestà* of Lucca, Pietrasanta was seen as a prize by Genoa, Lucca, Pisa and Florence, all of whom jostled for possession of its marble quarries and bronze foundries. Florence predictably won and Leo X (Giovanni de' Medici) took control in 1513, putting the town's famous quarries at the disposal of Michelangelo, who came here in 1518 to source marble for the facade of Florence's San Lorenzo. The artistic inclination of Pietrasanta dates from this time, and today it is the home of many artists, including internationally lauded Colombian-born sculptor Fernando Botero, whose work can be seen here.

⊙ Sights

From Pietrasantra train station (Piazza della Stazione) head straight across Piazza Carducci to the old city gate and onto the central square, **Piazza del Duomo**.

Duomo di San Martino   CATHEDRAL
(Piazza del Duomo; ☉variable) It is impossible to miss Pietrasanta's attractive cathedral, dating from 1256, on the central square. Its distinctive 36m-tall, red-brick bell tower is actually unfinished; the red brick was meant to have a marble cladding.

Chiesa di Sant'Agostino   CHURCH
(Piazza del Duomo; ☉variable) The far end of Piazza del Duomo is dominated by the 13th-century stone hulk of this deconsecrated church. Once dedicated to St Augustine, the Romanesque space hosts seasonal art exhibitions today.

Museo dei Bozzetti   MUSEUM
(☑0584 79 55 00; www.museodeibozzetti.it; Via Sant'Agostino 1; ☉9am-1pm & 2-7pm Tue-Fri, 2-7pm Sat, 4-7pm Sun) **FREE** Inside the convent adjoining Chiesa di Sant'Agostino dozens of moulds of famous sculptures cast or carved in Pietrasanta are showcased by this small museum.

Via della Rocca   VIEWPOINT
(Piazza del Duomo) Next to Chiesa di Sant'Agostino, a steep path known as Via della Rocca leads up to what remains of Piatrasanta's ancient fortifications. The crenellated city walls date to the early 1300s and what remains of **Palazzo Guinigi** was built as a residence for *signore* of Lucca, Paolo Guinigi, in 1408. Views of the city and the deep-blue Mediterranean beyond are predictably worth the short climb.

🛏 Sleeping & Eating

Le Camere di Filippo   B&B €€
(☑0584 7 00 10; www.filippolondon.it; Via Stagio Stagi 22; d €120-150; 🅿✳@🛜) A fabulous address with two kitchens and four fantastic rooms, each with a different colour scheme and crisp design.

Filippo   TUSCAN €€
(☑0584 7 00 10; http://ristorantefilippo.com; Via Stagio Stagi 22; meals €40; ☉12.30-2.30pm & 7.30pm-2am, closed Mon winter) 🍴 This exceptional foodie address never disappoints. From the homemade bread (all six or so varieties) and focaccia brought warm to your table throughout the course of your meal, to the contemporary fabric on the walls, giant wicker lampshades and modern open kitchen, this bistro is chic. Cuisine is seasonal and as creative as the interior design.

🍷 Drinking

L'Enoteca Marcucci   WINE BAR
(☑0584 79 19 62; www.enotecamarcucci.it; Via Garibaldi 40; ☉10am-1pm & 5pm-1am Tue-Sun) Taste fine Tuscan wine on bar stools at high wooden tables or beneath big parasols on the street outside. Whichever you pick, the distinctly funky, artsy spirit of Pietrasanta's best-loved *enoteca* enthrals.

Ever since its glory days as an ancient superpower, Rome has been astonishing visitors: its museums and basilicas showcase some of Europe's most celebrated masterpieces. But nothing can capture the sheer elation of experiencing Rome's operatic streets, baroque piazzas and colourful neighbourhood markets.

Rome & Lazio

ROME

POP 2.86 MILLION

According to myth, Rome was founded on the Palatino (Palatine Hill) by Romulus, twin brother of Remus and son of Mars, god of war. Historians offer a more prosaic version of events, claiming that Romulus became the first king of Rome on 21 April 753 BC. By AD 100 Rome had a population of 1.5 million and was the undisputed *caput mundi* (capital of the world). The cityscape reflects its rise and fall over the centuries, and its museums and basilicas showcase some of Europe's most celebrated masterpieces.

◎ Sights

Colosseum   RUIN
(Map p105; Colosseo; ☑ 06 3996 7700; www.coop culture.it; Piazza del Colosseo; adult/reduced incl Roman Forum & Palatino €12/7.50; ⊙ 8.30am-1hr before sunset; Ⓜ Colosseo) Originally known as the Flavian Amphitheatre, the 50,000-seat Colosseum is the most thrilling of Rome's ancient sights. It was here that gladiators met in mortal combat and where condemned prisoners fought wild beasts in front of baying, bloodthirsty crowds. Visit in the early morning to avoid the crowds.

Palatino   ARCHAEOLOGICAL SITE
(Map p105; Palatine Hill; ☑ 06 3996 7700; www. coopculture.it; Via di San Gregorio 30 & Via Sacra;

adult/reduced incl Colosseum & Roman Forum €12/7.50; ⊙ 8.30am-1hr before sunset; Ⓜ Colosseo) The Palatino is an atmospheric area of towering pine trees, majestic ruins and memorable views. It was here that Romulus supposedly founded the city in 753 BC, and Rome's emperors lived in unabashed luxury. Look out for the **stadio** (stadium), the ruins of the **Domus Flavia** (imperial palace), and grandstand views over the Roman Forum from the **Orti Farnesiani**.

Roman Forum   ARCHAEOLOGICAL SITE
(Map p105; Foro Romano; ☑ 06 3996 7700; www. coopculture.it; Largo della Salara Vecchia & Via Sacra; adult/reduced incl Colosseum & Palatino €12/7.50; ⊙ 8.30am-1hr before sunset; ▣ Via dei Fori Imperiali) An impressive – if rather confusing – sprawl of ruins, the Roman Forum was ancient Rome's showpiece centre, a grandiose district of temples, basilicas and vibrant public spaces. The site, which was originally an Etruscan burial ground, was first developed in the 7th century BC, growing over time to become the social, political and commercial hub of the Roman empire.

Pantheon   CHURCH
(Map p105; Piazza della Rotonda; ⊙ 8.30am-7.30pm Mon-Sat, 9am-6pm Sun; ▣ Largo di Torre Argentina) The Pantheon is one of Rome's most iconic

sights. A striking 2000-year-old temple, now a church, it is the city's best-preserved ancient monument and one of the most influential buildings in the Western world. The greying, pock-marked exterior might look its age, but inside it's a different story, and it's a unique and exhilarating experience to pass through the towering bronze doors and have your vision directed upwards to the breathtaking dome.

Piazza di Spagna & the Spanish Steps
PIAZZA

(Map p105; Ⓜ Spagna) A magnet for visitors since the 18th century, the Spanish Steps (Scalinata della Trinità dei Monti) provide a perfect people-watching perch and you'll almost certainly find yourself taking stock here at some point.

Trevi Fountain
FOUNTAIN

(Map p105; Fontana di Trevi; Piazza di Trevi; Ⓜ Barberini) The Fontana di Trevi, scene of Anita Ekberg's dip in *La Dolce Vita*, is a flamboyant baroque ensemble of mythical figures, and wild horses. It takes up the entire side of the 17th-century Palazzo Poli. A Fendi-sponsored restoration finished in 2015, and the fountain now gleams brighter than it has for years.

The tradition is to toss a coin into the water, thus ensuring that you'll return to Rome.

St Peter's Basilica
BASILICA

(Map p100; Basilica di San Pietro; www.vatican. va; St Peter's Sq; ⊙ 7am-7pm summer, to 6.30pm winter; Ⓜ Ottaviano-San Pietro) FREE In this city of outstanding churches, none can hold a candle to St Peter's (Basilica di San Pietro), Italy's largest, richest and most spectacular basilica. Built atop an earlier 4th-century church, it was completed in 1626 after 120 years' construction. Its lavish interior contains many spectacular works of art, including three of Italy's most celebrated masterpieces: Michelangelo's *Pietà*, his soaring dome, and Bernini's 29m-high baldachin over the papal altar.

Expect queues and note that strict dress codes are enforced, so no shorts, miniskirts or bare shoulders.

ROME & LAZIO ROME

Colosseum

Rome

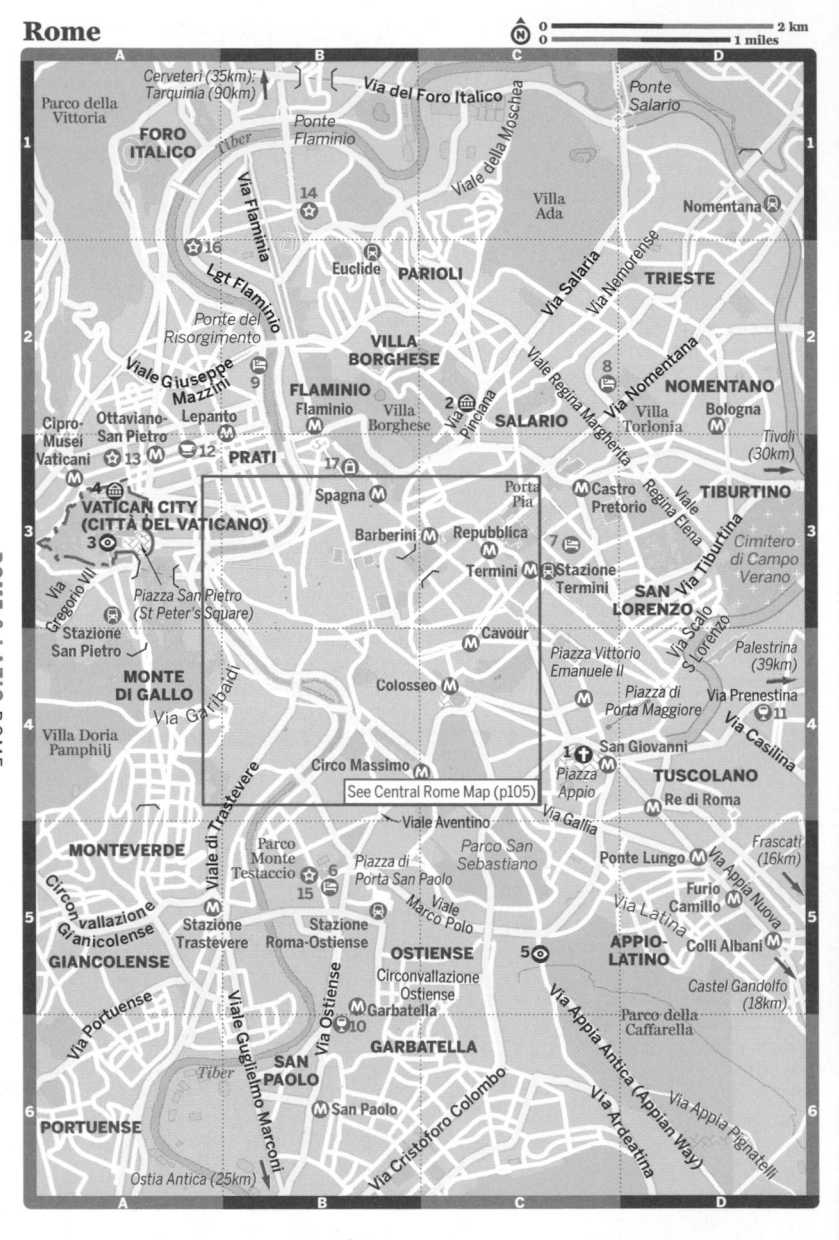

Vatican Museums   MUSEUM
(Map p100; Musei Vaticani; ☎06 6988 4676; http://
mv.vatican.va; Viale Vaticano; adult/reduced €16/8,
last Sun of month free; ⊙9am-4pm Mon-Sat,
9am-12.30pm last Sun of month; ⓜOttaviano-San
Pietro) Visiting the Vatican Museums is a

thrilling and unforgettable experience. The highlight is the Michelangelo-decorated Sistine Chapel, but with some 7km of exhibitions and more masterpieces than many small countries, there's enough art on display to keep you busy for years. Housing it

Rome

all is the 5.5-hectare Palazzo Apostolico Vaticano, which also serves as the pope's official residence.

Museo Nazionale Romano: Palazzo Massimo alle Terme   MUSEUM

(Map p105; ☑ 06 3996 7700; www.coopculture. it; Largo di Villa Peretti 1; adult/reduced €7/3.50; ⊕ 9am-7.45pm Tue-Sun; Ⓜ Termini) One of Rome's great unheralded museums, this is a fabulous treasure trove of classical art. The ground and 1st floors are devoted to sculpture with some breathtaking pieces – check out the *Pugile* (Boxer), a 2nd-century-BC Greek bronze; the graceful 2nd-century-BC *Ermafrodite dormiente* (Sleeping Hermaphrodite); and the idealised *Il Discobolo* (Discus Thrower). It's the magnificent and vibrantly coloured frescoes on the 2nd floor, however, that are the undisputed highlight.

Basilica di Santa Maria in Trastevere   BASILICA

(Map p105; Piazza Santa Maria in Trastevere; ⊕ 7.30am-9pm; ☐ Viale di Trastevere, ☐ Viale di Trastevere) Nestled in a quiet corner of Trastevere's focal square, this is said to be the oldest church dedicated to the Virgin Mary in Rome. In its original form it dates to the early 3rd century, but a major 12th-century

makeover saw the addition of a Romanesque bell tower and glittering facade. The portico came later, added by Carlo Fontana in 1702.

Inside, the 12th-century mosaics are the headline feature.

Basilica di San Giovanni in Laterano   BASILICA

(Map p100; Piazza di San Giovanni in Laterano 4; basilica/cloister free/€5; ⊕ 7am-6.30pm, cloister 9am-6pm; Ⓜ San Giovanni) For a thousand years this monumental cathedral was the most important church in Christendom. Commissioned by Constantine and consecrated in AD 324, it was the first Christian basilica built in the city and, until the late 14th century, was the pope's main place of worship. It's still Rome's official cathedral and the pope's seat as the bishop of Rome.

The basilica has been revamped several times, most notably by Borromini in the 17th century, and by Alessandro Galilei, who added the immense white facade in 1735.

Museo e Galleria Borghese   MUSEUM

(Map p100; ☑ 06 3 28 10; www.galleriaborghese. it; Piazzale del Museo Borghese 5; adult/reduced €11/6.50; ⊕ 9am-7pm Tue-Sun; ☐ Via Pinciana) If you only have the time (or inclination) for one art gallery in Rome, make it this one. Housing what's often referred to as the 'queen of all private art collections', it boasts paintings by Caravaggio, Raphael, and Titian, as well as some sensational sculptures by Bernini. Highlights abound, but look out for Bernini's *Ratto di Proserpina* (Rape of Proserpina) and Canova's *Venere vincitrice* (Venus Victrix).

To limit numbers, visitors are admitted at two-hourly intervals, so you'll need to pre-book your ticket and get an entry time.

Via Appia Antica   HISTORIC SITE

(Map p105; Appian Way; ☑ 06 513 53 16; www. parcoappiaantica.it; bike hire hr/day €3/15; ⊕ Info Point 9.30am-1pm & 2-5.30pm Mon-Fri, 9.30am-6.30pm Sat & Sun, to 5pm winter; ☐ Via Appia Antica) Named after consul Appius Claudius Caecus who laid the first 90km section in 312 BC, ancient Rome's *regina viarum* (queen of roads) was extended in 190 BC to reach Brindisi on Italy's southern Adriatic coast. Via Appia Antica has long been one of Rome's most exclusive addresses, a beautiful cobbled thoroughfare flanked by grassy fields, Roman structures and towering pine trees. Most splendid of the ancient houses was Villa dei Quintilli, so desirable that emperor Commodus murdered its owners and took it for himself.

 Courses

Roman Kitchen
COOKING

(Map p105; ☑06 678 57 59; www.italiangourmet.com; per day €200) Cookery writer Diane Seed *(The Top One Hundred Pasta Sauces)* runs cooking courses from her kitchen in Palazzo Doria Pamphilj. There are one-day, two-day, three-day and week-long courses costing €200 per day and €1000 per week.

Vino Roma
WINE COURSE

(Map p105; ☑328 4874497; www.vinoroma.com; Via in Selci 84/G; 2hr tastings per person €50) With beautifully appointed 1000-year-old cellars and a chic tasting studio, Vino Roma guides novices and experts in tasting wine, under the knowledgeable stewardship of sommelier Hande Leimer and his expert team. Tastings are in English, but German, Japanese, Italian and Turkish sessions are available on special request. It also offers a wine-and-cheese dinner (€60), with snacks, cheeses and cold cuts to accompany the wines, and bespoke three-hour food tours.

☞ Tours

Roman Guy
TOUR

(http://theromanguy.com) A professional set-up that organises a wide range of group and private tours. Packages, led by English-speaking experts, include early-bird visits to the Vatican Museums (US$84), foodie tours of Trastevere and the Jewish Ghetto (US$84), and a bar hop through the historic centre's cocktail bars.

Eating Italy Food Tours
FOOD TOUR

(www.eatingitalyfoodtours.com; €75; ☉daily) This cheery food tour company is run by American ex-pat Kenny Dunn, and offers informative four-hour tours around the Testaccio (the heartland of traditional Roman cooking), or Trastevere, with chances to taste 12 delicacies on the way. There are a maximum of 12 people to a tour.

Top Bike Rental & Tours
BICYCLE TOUR

(Map p105; ☑06 488 28 93; www.topbikerental.com; Via Labicana 49; ☉10am-7pm) Offers a series of bike tours throughout the city, including a four-hour 16km exploration of the city centre (€45) and an all-day 30km ride through Via Appia Antica and environs (€79). Out-of-town tours take in Castel Gandolfo, Civita di Bagnoregio and Orvieto.

🛌 Sleeping

Beehive
HOSTEL €

(Map p100; ☑06 4470 4553; www.the-beehive.com; Via Marghera 8; dm €25-35, s €50-80, d €90-100, without bathroom s €60-70, d €70-80, tr €95-105; ❄ 🛜; Ⓜ Termini) ✎ More boutique chic than backpacker dive, the Beehive is Rome's best hostel; book well ahead. There's a spotless, eight-person mixed dorm or six private double rooms, some with air-con. Original artworks and funky modular furniture add colour, plus there's a cafe. Some bright, well-

---

ROMULUS & REMUS, ROME'S LEGENDARY TWINS

The most famous of Rome's many legends is the story of Romulus and Remus and the city's foundation on 21 April 753 BC.

According to myth, Romulus and Remus were the children of the vestal virgin, Rhea Silva, and Mars, god of war. While still babies they were set adrift on the Tiber to escape a death penalty imposed by their great-uncle Amulius, who was battling with their grandfather Numitor for control of the city of Alba Longa. However, they were discovered near the Palatino by a she-wolf, who suckled them until a shepherd, Faustulus, found and raised them.

Years later the twins decided to found a city on the site where they'd been saved. They didn't know where this was, so they consulted the omens. Remus, standing on the Aventino, saw six vultures; his brother over on the Palatino saw 12. Romulus claimed the Palatino as the right spot and began building, much to the outrage of his brother. The two subsequently argued and Romulus killed Remus. Romulus continued building and soon had a city. To populate it he created a refuge on the Capitoline, Aventino, Celian and Quirinale hills, to which a ragtag population of criminals, ex-slaves and outlaws soon decamped. However, the city still needed women. To remedy this, Romulus invited everyone in the surrounding country to celebrate the Festival of Consus (21 August). As the spectators watched the festival games, Romulus and his men pounced and abducted all the women, an infamous act that went down in history as the Rape of the Sabine Women.

cared-for off-site rooms, sharing communal bathrooms and kitchen, are another bargain (single €40 to €50, double €60 to €80).

Althea Inn
B&B €

(Map p100; ☑ 339 4353717, 06 9893 2666; www.altheainn.com; Via dei Conciatori 9; d €70-125; M Piramide) In a workaday apartment block, this friendly B&B offers superb value for money and easy access to Testaccio's bars, clubs and restaurants. Its spacious, light-filled rooms sport a modish look white walls and tasteful modern furniture. Each also has a small terrace.

Palm Gallery Hotel
HOTEL €€

(Map p100; ☑ 06 6478 1859; www.palmgalleryhotel.com; Via delle Alpi 15d; s €100-120, d €100-210; ❄ 🛜; 🚍 Via Nomentana, 🚍 Viale Regina Margherita) Housed in an early-20th-century villa, this gorgeous hotel sports an eclectic look that effortlessly blends African and Middle Eastern art with original art-deco furniture, exposed brickwork and hand-painted tiles. Rooms are individually decorated, with the best offering views over the wisteria and thick greenery in the surrounding streets.

Residenza Maritti
GUESTHOUSE €€

(Map p105; ☑ 06 678 82 33; www.residenzamaritti.com; Via Tor de' Conti 17; s €50-120, d €80-170, tr €100-190; ❄ 🛜; M Cavour) Boasting stunning views over the forums, this gem has rooms spread over several floors. Some are bright and modern, others are cosy in feel with antiques and family furniture. There's no breakfast but you can use a fully equipped kitchen.

Arco del Lauro
B&B €€

(Map p105; ☑ 346 2443212, 9am-2pm 06 9/84 0350; www.arcodellauro.it; Via Arco de' Tolomei 27; s €72-132, d €132-145; ❄ 🛜; 🚍 Viale di Trastevere, 🚍 Viale di Trastevere) A real find, this fab six-room B&B occupies a centuries-old *palazzo* (mansion) on a narrow cobbled street. Its gleaming white rooms combine rustic charm with a modern low-key look and comfortable beds. The owners extend a warm welcome and are always ready to help.

Villa Laetitia
BOUTIQUE HOTEL €€€

(Map p100; ☑ 06 322 67 76; www.villalaetitia.com; Lungotevere delle Armi 22; r €200-280, ste €500; ❄ 🛜; 🚍 Lungotevere delle Armi) Villa Laetitia is a stunning boutique hotel in a riverside art-nouveau villa. Its 20 rooms, each individually designed by Anna Venturini Fendi of the famous fashion house, marry modern design touches with vintage pieces and

> #### APERITIVO ROMAN STYLE
>
> Originally a northern Italian custom, the *aperitivo* is now an established part of Rome's social scene and many bars serve lavish buffets between 6pm and 9pm. To partake, order a drink – there's usually a standard charge of around €8 to €10 – and dig in.

rare finds, such as an original Picasso in the Garden Room.

Villa Spalletti Trivelli
HOTEL €€€

(Map p105; ☑ 06 4890 7934; www.villaspalletti.it; Via Piacenza 4; r €450-620; ❄ @ 🛜; M Spagna) With 12 rooms in a glorious mansion in central Rome, Villa Spalletti Trivelli was built by Gabriella Rasponi, widow of Italian senator Count Venceslao Spalletti Triveli and the niece of Carolina Bonaparte (Napoleon's sister). It offers a sojourn in a stately home; rooms are soberly and elegantly decorated, and the sitting rooms are hung with 16th-century tapestries or lined by antique books. There's also a basement spa.

Donna Camilla Savelli
HOTEL €€€

(Map p105; ☑ 06 58 88 61; www.hoteldonnacamillasavelli.com; Via Garibaldi 27; d €165-250; ❄ @ 🛜; 🚍 Viale di Trastevere, 🚍 Viale di Trastevere) It's seldom you have such an exquisite opportunity as to stay in a converted convent that was designed by baroque genius Borromini. It's been beautifully updated; muted colours complement the serene concave and convex curves of the architecture, and service is excellent. The pricier of the 78 rooms overlook the lovely cloister garden or have views of Rome, and are decorated with antiques – it's worth forking out that bit extra.

✖ Eating

Rome teems with trattorias, *ristoranti*, pizzerias, *enoteche* (wine bars serving food) and gelaterie. Excellent places dot the *centro storico* (historic centre), Trastevere, Prati, Testaccio and San Lorenzo. The area around Termini has quite a few substandard restaurants, as does the Vatican, which is packed with tourist traps.

Supplizio
FAST FOOD €

(Map p105; Via dei Banchi Vecchi 143; supplì €3-5; ⏱ noon-4pm Mon-Sat plus 5.30-10pm Mon-Thu, to 11pm Fri & Sat; 🚍 Corso Vittorio Emanuele II) Rome's favourite snack, the *supplì* (a fried croquette filled with rice, tomato sauce and mozzarella), gets a gourmet makeover at this elegant new streetfood joint. Sit back on the vintage leather sofa and dig into the classic article – or throw the boat out and try something different, maybe a mildly spicy fish *supplì* stuffed with anchovies, tuna, parsley, and just a hint of orange.

Cafè Cafè
BISTRO €

(Map p105; ☑06 700 87 43; www.cafecafebistrot. it; Via dei Santissimi Quattro Coronati 44; meals €15-20; ⊙9.30am-11pm; ☒Via di San Giovanni in Laterano) Cosy, relaxed and welcoming, this cafe-bistro is a far cry from the usual impersonal eateries in the Colosseum area. With its rustic wooden tables, butternut walls and wine bottles, it's a charming spot to recharge your batteries over tea and homemade cake, a light lunch or laid-back dinner. There's also brunch on Sundays.

Terre e Domus
LAZIO CUISINE €€

(Map p105; ☑06 6994 0273; Via Foro Traiano 82-4; meals €30; ⊙7.30am-12.30am Mon-Sat; ☒Via dei Fori Imperiali) This modern white-and-glass restaurant is the best option in the touristy Forum area. Overlooking the Colonna di Traiano, it serves a menu of traditional staples, all made with ingredients sourced from the surrounding Lazio region, and a thoughtful selection of regional wines. Lunchtime can be busy but it quietens down in the evening.

La Ciambella
ITALIAN €€

(Map p105; www.laciambellaroma.com; Via dell'Arco della Ciambella 20; fixed-price lunch menus €10-25, meals €30; ⊙7.30am-midnight; ☒Largo di Torre Argentina) From breakfast pastries and lunchtime pastas to afternoon tea, Neapolitan pizzas and aperitif cocktails, this all-day eatery is a top find. Central but as yet undiscovered by the tourist hordes, it's a spacious, light-filled spot set over the ruins of the Terme di Agrippa, visible through transparent floor panels. The mostly traditional food is spot on, and the atmosphere laid back and friendly.

Enoteca Regionale
Palatium
RISTORANTE, WINE BAR €€€

(Map p105; ☑06 692 02 132; Via Frattina 94; meals €55; ⊙11am-11pm Mon-Sat, closed Aug; ☒Via del Corso) A rich showcase of regional bounty, run by the Lazio Regional Food Authority, this sleek wine bar serves excellent local specialities, such as *porcetto* (pork roasted with herbs) or *gnocchi alla romana con crema da zucca* (potato dumplings

Roman-style with cream of pumpkin), as well as an impressive array of Lazio wines (try lesser-known drops such as Aleatico). *Aperitivo* is a good bet, too.

Open Colonna
ITALIAN €€€

(Map p105; ☑06 4782 2641; www.antonellocolonna. it; Via Milano 9a; meals €20-80; ⊙12.30-3.30pm Tue-Sun, 8-11.30pm Tue-Sat; ☒Via Nazionale) Spectacularly set at the back of Palazzo delle Esposizioni, superchef Antonello Colonna's superb restaurant is tucked onto a mezzanine floor under an extraordinary glass roof. The cuisine is New Roman: innovative takes on traditional dishes, cooked with wit and flair. The best thing? There's a more basic but still delectable fixed two-course lunch for €16, and Saturday and Sunday brunch is €30, served in the dramatic, glass-ceilinged hall, with a terrace for sunny days.

🍷 Drinking & Nightlife

Rome has plenty of drinking venues, ranging from traditional *enoteche* (wine bars) and streetside cafes to cool cocktail bars, pubs and counterculture hang-outs. During the day people usually head to bars for a quick coffee, while early evening sees the city's hipsters turn out for the evening *aperitivo*.

0,75
BAR

(Map p105; www.075roma.com; Via dei Cerchi 65; ⊙11am-2am; 🛜; ☒Via dei Cerchi) This welcoming bar on the Circo Massimo is good for a lingering drink, an *aperitivo* (6.30pm onwards) or a light meal (mains €6 to €13.50, salads €5.50 to €7.50). It's a friendly place with a laid-back vibe, an attractive exposed-brick look and cool tunes.

Barnum Cafe
CAFE

(Map p105; www.barnumcafe.com; Via del Pellegrino 87; ⊙9am-10pm Mon, 8.30am-2am Tue-Sat; 🛜; ☒Corso Vittorio Emanuele II) A relaxed, friendly spot to check your email over a freshly squeezed orange juice or spend a pleasant hour reading a newspaper on one of the tatty old armchairs in the white bare-brick interior. Come evenings and the scene is cocktails, smooth tunes and coolly dressed-down locals.

No.Au
BAR

(Map p105; Piazza Montevecchio 16; ⊙6pm-1am Tue-Thu, noon-1am Fri-Sun; ☒Corso del Rinascimento) Opening onto a charming *centro storico* piazza, No.Au – pronounced Know How – is a cool bistrot-bar set-up. Like many fashionable bars, it's big on beer and offers

Central Rome

Central Rome

a knowledgeable list of artisanal craft brews, as well as local wines and a small but select food menu.

Sciascia Caffè
CAFE

(Map p100; Via Fabio Massimo 80/A; ⊙ 7.30am-6.30pm Mon-Sat; Ⓜ Ottaviano–San Pietro) The timeless elegance of this polished cafe is perfectly suited to the exquisite coffee it makes. There are various options but nothing can beat the *caffè eccellente,* a velvety smooth espresso served in a delicate cup that has been lined with melted chocolate. The result is nothing short of magnificent.

Il Tiaso
BAR

(Map p100; ☏ 06 4547 4625; www.iltiaso.com; Via Perugia 20; 🛜; ⧉ Circonvallazione Casilina) Think living room with zebra-print chairs, walls of indie art, Lou Reed biographies shelved between wine bottles, and 30-something owner Gabriele playing his latest New York Dolls album to neo-beatnik chicks, corduroy professors and the odd neighbourhood dog. Well-priced wine, an intimate chilled vibe, and regular live music.

Goa
CLUB

(Map p100; ☏ 06 574 82 77; www.goaclub.com; Via Libetta 13; ⊙ 11.30pm-4.30am Thu-Sat; Ⓜ Garbatella) Goa is Rome's serious super-club, with international names, a fashion-forward crowd, podium dancers and heavies on the door.

☆ Entertainment

Auditorium Parco della Musica
CONCERT VENUE

(Map p100; ☏ 06 8024 1281; www.auditorium.com; Viale Pietro de Coubertin 30; ⧉ Viale Tiziano) The hub of Rome's thriving cultural scene, the Auditorium is the capital's premier concert venue and one of Europe's most popular arts centres. Its three concert halls offer superb acoustics, and, together with a 3000-seat open-air arena, stage everything from classical-music concerts to jazz gigs, public lectures, and film screenings.

Teatro Olimpico
THEATRE

(Map p100; ☏ 06 326 59 91; www.teatroolimpico.it; Piazza Gentile da Fabriano 17; ⧉ Piazza Mancini) Home to the **Accademia Filarmonica Romana** (www.filarmonica romana.org), a classical-music organisation whose past members have included Rossini, Donizetti and Verdi, this theatre offers a varied program of classical and chamber music, opera, ballet, one-person shows and comedies.

Teatro dell'Opera di Roma
OPERA

(Map p105; ☏ 06 481 70 03; www.operaroma.it; Piazza Beniamino Gigli; ballet €12-80, opera €17-150; ⊙ 9am-5pm Tue-Sat, to 1.30pm Sun; Ⓜ Repubblica) Rome's premier opera house boasts a plush-and-gilt interior, a Fascist 1920s exterior and an impressive history: it premiered Puccini's *Tosca,* and Maria Callas once sang here. Opera and ballet performances are staged between September and June.

Alexanderplatz
JAZZ

(Map p100; ☏ 06 3972 1867; www.alexanderplatz jazzclub.com; Via Ostia 9; ⊙ 8.30pm-2am, concerts 9.45pm; Ⓜ Ottaviano–San Pietro) Small, intimate and underground, Rome's most celebrated jazz club draws top Italian and international performers and a respectful cosmopolitan crowd. Book a table for the best stage views or if you want to dine to the tunes. Check the website for upcoming gigs.

Big Mama
BLUES

(Map p105; ☏ 06 581 25 51; www.bigmama.it; Vicolo di San Francesco a Ripa 18; ⊙ 9pm-1.30am, shows 10.30pm, closed Jun-Sep; ⧉ Viale di Trastevere, ⧉ Viale di Trastevere) Head to this cramped Trastevere basement for a mellow night of Eternal City blues. A long-standing venue, it also stages jazz, funk, soul and R&B, as well as popular Italian cover bands.

ConteStaccio
LIVE MUSIC

(Map p100; www.contestaccio.com; Via di Monte Testaccio 65b; ⊙ 7pm-4am Tue-Sun; ⧉ Via Galvani) With an under-the-stars terrace and cool, arched interior, ConteStaccio is one of the top venues on the Testaccio clubbing strip. It's something of a multi-purpose outfit with a cocktail bar, a pizzeria and a restaurant, but is best known for its daily concerts. Gigs by emerging groups set the tone, spanning indie, rock, acoustic, funk and electronic.

🛍 Shopping

Confetteria Moriondo & Gariglio
FOOD

(Map p105; Via del Piè di Marmo 21-22; ⊙ 9am-7.30pm Mon-Sat; ⧉ Via del Corso) Roman poet Trilussa was so smitten with this historic chocolate shop – established by the Torinese confectioners to the royal house of Savoy – that he dedicated several sonnets to it. And we agree, it's a gem. Many of the bonbons and handmade chocolates laid out in ceremonial splendour in the glass cabinets are still prepared according to original 19th-century recipes.

Ibiz – Artigianato in Cuoio ACCESSORIES
(Map p105; Via dei Chiavari 39; ⊙9.30am-7.30pm Mon-Sat; 🚋Corso Vittorio Emanuele II) In their diminutive workshop, Elisa Nepi and her father craft exquisite, well-priced leather goods, including wallets, bags, belts and sandals, in simple but classy designs and myriad colours. You can pick up a belt for about €35, while for a bag you should bank on at least €110.

Bottega di Marmoraro ARTS
(Map p100; Via Margutta 53b; ⊙8am-7.30pm Mon-Sat; 🅼Flaminio) A particularly charismatic hole-in-the-wall shop lined with marble carvings, where you can get marble tablets engraved with any inscription you like (€15). Peer inside at lunchtime and you might see the cheerfully quizzical *marmoraro* himself, Enrico Fiorentini, cooking pasta for his lunch next to the log fire.

Danielle SHOES
(Map p105; 🗐06 679 24 67; Via Frattina 85a; ⊙10.30am-7.30pm; 🅼Spagna) If you're female and in need of an Italian shoe fix, this is an essential stop on your itinerary. It sells both classic and fashionable styles – foxy heels, boots and ballet pumps – at extremely reasonable prices. Shoes are of soft leather and come in myriad colours.

Tina Sondergaard CLOTHING
(Map p105; 🗐334 3850799; Via del Boschetto 1d; ⊙3-7.30pm Mon, 10.30am-7.30pm Tue-Sat, closed Aug; 🅼Cavour) Sublimely cut and whimsically retro, these handmade threads are a hit with female fashion cognoscenti, including Italian rock star Carmen Consoli and the city's theatre and TV crowd. You can have adjustments made (included in the price), and dresses cost around €140.

Porta Portese Market MARKET
(Map p105; Piazza Porta Portese; ⊙6am-2pm Sun; 🚋Viale di Trastevere, 🚋Viale di Trastevere) To see another side of Rome, head to this mammoth flea market. With thousands of stalls selling everything from rare books and fell-off-a-lorry bikes to Peruvian shawls and MP3 players, it's crazily busy and a lot of fun. Keep your valuables safe and wear your haggling hat.

ⓘ Orientation

Rome is a sprawling city but the centre is relatively compact and most sights are concentrated in the area between Stazione Termini, the city's main transport hub, and the Vatican to the west. Halfway between the two, the Pantheon and Piazza Navona lie at the heart of the *centro storico*, while to the south, the Colosseum lords it over the city's great ancient ruins: the Roman Forum and Palatino. On the west bank of the Tiber, St Peter's Basilica trumpets the presence of the Vatican.

Distances are not great so walking is often the best way to get around.

ⓘ Information

MEDICAL SERVICES

For problems that don't require hospital treatment, call the **Guardia Medica** (🗐06 884 01 13; Via Mantova 44; ⊙24 hr).

More convenient, if you have insurance and can afford to pay up front, is to call a doctor for a home visit. Try the **International Medical Centre** (🗐06 488 23 71; Via Firenze 47; GP call-out & treatment fee €140, 8pm-9am & weekends €200; ⊙24hr).

Pharmacists will serve prescriptions and can provide basic medical advice. Night pharmacies are listed in daily newspapers and in pharmacy windows.

TOURIST INFORMATION

For phone enquiries, the Comune di Roma runs a free multilingual **tourist information line** (🗐06 06 08; ⊙9am-9pm).

USEFUL WEBSITES

060608 (www.060608.it) Provides information on sites, accommodation, shows, transport.

Coop Culture (www.coopculture.it) Information and ticketing for Rome's monuments, museums and galleries.

In Rome Now (www.inromenow.com) Savvy internet magazine compiled by two American expats.

Turismo Roma (www.turismoroma.it) Rome's official tourist website. Lists accommodation options, upcoming events and more.

Vatican (www.vatican.va) The Vatican's website.

ⓘ Getting There & Away

AIR

Rome's main international airport, Leonardo da Vinci (p121), better known as Fiumicino, is on the coast 30km west of the city.

MUSEUM DISCOUNT CARDS

Serious museum-goers should consider:

Classic Roma Pass (€36; valid for three days) Provides free admission to two museums or sites, as well as reduced entry to extra sites, unlimited city transport and discounted entry to other exhibitions and events.

48-hour Roma Pass (€28; valid for 48 hours) Gives free admission to one museum or site and then as per the Classic pass.

Archaeologia Card (adult/reduced €27.50/17.50; valid for seven days) Covers the Colosseum, Palatino, Roman Forum, Terme di Caracalla, Palazzo Altemps, Palazzo Massimo alle Terme, Terme di Diocleziano, Crypta Balbi, Mausoleo di Cecilia Metella and Villa dei Quintili.

These are all available at participating museums or online at www.coopculture.it. You can also get the Roma Pass at tourist information points.

The much smaller **Ciampino Airport** (☑ 06 6 59 51; www.adr.it/ciampino), 15km southeast of the city centre, is the hub for European low-cost carrier Ryanair (p121).

CAR & MOTORCYCLE

Driving into central Rome is a challenge, involving traffic restrictions, one-way systems, a shortage of street parking and aggressive drivers.

Rome is circled by the *Grande Raccordo Anulare* (GRA) to which all autostradas (motorways) connect, including the main A1 north–south artery (the Autostrada del Sole) and the A12, which runs to Civitavecchia and Fiumicino airport.

Car Hire

Rental cars are available at the airport and Stazione Termini.

Avis (☑ 199 100 133; www.avisautonoleggio.it)
Europcar (☑ 199 30 70 30; www.europcar.it)
Hertz (☑ 02 6943 0019; www.hertz.it)
Maggiore National (☑ 199 151 120; www.maggiore.it)

Access & Parking

➜ Most of the historic centre is closed to unauthorised traffic from 6.30am to 6pm Monday to Friday, from 2pm to 6pm (10am to 7pm in some places) Saturday, and from 11pm to 3am Friday and Saturday. Evening restrictions also apply in Trastevere, San Lorenzo, Monti and Testaccio, typically from 9.30pm or 11pm to 3am on Fridays and Saturdays.

➜ All streets accessing the 'Limited Traffic Zone' (ZTL) are monitored by electronic-access detection devices. If you're staying in this zone, contact your hotel. For further information, check www.agenziamobilita.roma.it.

➜ Blue lines denote pay-and-display parking – get tickets from meters (coins only) and *tabaccaio* (tobaconnists).

➜ Expect to pay up to €1.20 per hour between 8am and 8pm (11pm in some places). After 8pm (or 11pm) parking is free until 8am the next morning.

➜ Traffic wardens are vigilant and fines are not uncommon. If your car gets towed away, call ☑ 06 6769 2303.

➜ There's a comprehensive list of car parks at www.060608.it – click on the Transports tab, then Car parks.

PUBLIC TRANSPORT

Rome's public transport system includes buses, trams, metro and a suburban train network.

Metro

➜ Rome has two main metro lines, A (orange) and B (blue), which cross at Termini. A branch line, 'B1', serves the northern suburbs, and a line C runs through the southeastern outskirts, but you're unlikely to need these.

➜ Trains run between 5.30am and 11.30pm (to 1.30am on Fridays and Saturdays).

➜ All stations on line B have wheelchair access except Circo Massimo, Colosseo and Cavour. On line A, Ottaviano–San Pietro and Termini are equipped with lifts.

➜ Take line A for the Trevi Fountain (Barberini), Spanish Steps (Spagna) and St Peter's (Ottaviano–San Pietro).

➜ Take line B for the Colosseum (Colosseo).

Bus & Tram

➜ Rome's buses and trams are run by **ATAC** (☑ 06 5 70 03; www.atac.roma.it).

➜ The main bus station is in front of Stazione Termini on Piazza dei Cinquecento, where there's an **information booth** (⊙ 7.30am-8pm).

➜ Other important hubs are at Largo di Torre Argentina and Piazza Venezia.

- Buses generally run from about 5.30am until midnight, with limited services throughout the night.
- Rome's night bus service comprises more than 25 lines, many of which pass Termini and/or Piazza Venezia. These buses are marked with an 'n' before the number and bus stops have a blue owl symbol. Departures are usually every 15 to 30 minutes between about 1am and 5am, but can be much less frequent.

TAXI

- Official licensed taxis are white with an ID number and *Roma Capitale* on the sides.
- Always go with the metered fare, never an arranged price (the set fares to/from the airports are exceptions).
- In town (within the ring road) flag fall is €3 between 6am and 10pm on weekdays and Saturdays, €4.50 on Sundays and holidays, and €6.50 between 10pm and 6am. Then it's €1.10 per kilometre. Official rates are posted in taxis and on www.agenziamobilita.roma.it.
- You can hail a taxi, but it's often easier to wait at a rank or phone for one. There are taxi ranks at the airports, Stazione Termini, Piazza della Repubblica, Piazza Barberini, Piazza di Spagna, the Pantheon, the Colosseum, Largo di Torre Argentina, Piazza Belli, Piazza Pio XII and Piazza del Risorgimento.
- You can book a taxi by phoning the Comune di Roma's automated taxi line on ☏ 06 06 09 or by calling a taxi company direct.
- Note that when you call for a cab, the meter is switched on straight away and you pay for the cost of the journey from wherever the driver receives the call.

La Capitale (☏ 06 49 94)
Pronto Taxi (☏ 06 66 45)
Radio 3570 (☏ 06 35 70; www.3570.it)
Samarcanda (☏ 06 55 51; www.samarcanda.lt)
Tevere (☏ 06 41 57)

LAZIO

With a capital like Rome, it's unsurprising that the rest of Lazio gets overlooked. But venture out of the city and you'll discover a region that's not only beautiful – verdant and hilly in the north, parched and rugged in the south – but also littered with historical and cultural gems.

Ostia Antica

One of Lazio's prize sights, the ruins of ancient Ostia are wonderfully complete, like a smaller version of Pompeii.

Founded in the 4th century BC, Ostia grew to become a great port and commercial centre with a population of around 50,000.

Decline set in after the fall of the Roman Empire, and by the 9th century the city had largely been abandoned, its citizens driven off by barbarian raids and outbreaks of malaria. Over subsequent centuries, it was plundered of marble and building materials and its ruins were gradually buried in river silt, hence their survival.

◉ Sights

**Scavi Archeologici di
Ostia Antica** ARCHAEOLOGICAL SITE
(☏ 06 5635 0215; www.ostiaantica.beniculturali.it; Viale dei Romagnoli 717; adult/reduced €10/6; ◷ 8.30am-6.15pm Tue-Sun summer, earlier closing winter) An easy train ride from Rome, Ostia Antica is one of Italy's most under-appreciated archaeological sites. The ruins of ancient Rome's main seaport are spread out and you'll need a few hours to do them justice. Highlights include the Terme di Nettuno (Baths of Neptune), a steeply stacked amphitheatre, and an ancient cafe, complete with bar and traces of the original menu frescoed on the wall.

Note that the site gets busy at weekends, but is much quieter on weekdays.

✕ Eating

Ristorante Monumento RISTORANTE €€
(☏ 06 565 00 21; www.ristorantemonumento.it; Piazza Umberto I 8; fixed-price lunch menu €14, meals €30; ◷ 12.30-3.30pm & 8-11pm) This historic restaurant started life in the 19th century, catering to the men working on reclaiming the local marshlands. Nowadays, it feeds sightseers fresh out of the nearby ruins, serving homemade pastas and excellent seafood. A fixed-price lunch menu is available Monday through Friday.

ℹ Getting There & Away

Take Via del Mare, which runs parallel to Via Ostiense, and follow signs for the *scavi* (excavations).

Tivoli

POP 56,460 / ELEV 235M

A summer retreat for ancient Romans and the Renaissance rich, the hilltop town of Tivoli is home to two Unesco World Heritage Sites: Villa Adriana, the sprawling estate of Emperor Hadrian, and the 16th-century

Villa d'Este, a Renaissance villa famous for its landscaped gardens and lavish fountains.

Information is available from the **tourist information point** (☑ 0774 31 35 36; Piazzale delle Nazione Unite; ⊘ 9.30am-5.30pm Tue-Sun) near where the bus arrives.

◉ Sights

Villa Adriana ARCHAEOLOGICAL SITE
(☑ 0774 38 27 33; www.villaadriana.beniculturali. it; adult/reduced €8/4; ⊘ 9am-1hr before sunset) The ruins of Hadrian's vast country villa, 5km outside Tivoli proper, are quite magnificent, easily on a par with anything you'll see in Rome. Built between AD 118 and 138, the villa was one of the largest in the ancient world, encompassing more than 120 hectares – of which about 40 are now open to the public. You'll need several hours to explore it.

Villa d'Este HISTORIC BUILDING, GARDENS
(☑ 0774 31 20 70; www.villadestetivoli.info; Piazza Trento; adult/reduced €8/4; ⊘ 8.30am-1hr before sunset Tue-Sun) In Tivoli's hilltop centre, the steeply terraced grounds of Villa d'Este are a superlative example of a Renaissance garden, complete with monumental fountains, elegant tree-lined avenues and landscaped grottoes. The villa, originally a Benedictine convent, was converted into a luxury retreat by Lucrezia Borgia's son, Cardinal Ippolito d'Este, in the late 16th century. It later provided inspiration for composer Franz Liszt, who stayed here between 1865 and 1886 and immortalised it in his 1877 piano composition *The Fountains of the Villa d'Este*.

✖ Eating

Trattoria del Falcone TRATTORIA €€
(☑ 0774 31 23 58; Via del Trevio 34; meals €30; ⊘ noon-4pm & 6.30-11pm) Near Villa d'Este, this cheerful, family-run trattoria has been serving pizzas, classic pastas, meat and seafood since 1918. Boasting exposed stone decor and a small internal courtyard, it's popular with both tourists and locals.

Sibilla RISTORANTE €€€
(☑ 0774 33 52 81; Via della Sibilla 50; meals €50; ⊘ 12.30-3pm & 7.30-10.30pm) With tables set out near two Roman temples and water cascading down the green river gorge below, the Sibilla's outdoor terrace sets a romantic stage for seasonally driven food and superlative wine.

❶ Getting There & Around

From Rome you can either take Via Tiburtina or the quicker Rome–L'Aquila autostrada (A24).

Cerveteri

POP 37,230 / ELEV 81M

35km northwest of Rome, Cerveteri is home to one of Italy's great Etruscan treasures – the Necropoli di Banditaccia. This ancient burial complex, now a Unesco World Heritage

Villa d'Este, Tivoli

LAZIO'S NORTHERN LAKES

North of Rome, Lazio's verdant landscape is pitted with volcanic lakes. The closest to the capital is **Lago di Bracciano**, a beautiful blue expanse surrounded by picturesque medieval towns. There's a popular lakeside beach at **Anguillara Sabazia** and you can visit a 15th-century castle, **Castello Odescalchi** (☑06 9980 4348; www.odescalchi.it; Via Gregorio VII 368; adult/reduced €8.50/6; ⊗10am-noon & 2-5pm Tue-Fri, 10am-6pm Sat & Sun summer, shorter hours winter), at **Bracciano**. The town lies 32km northwest of Tome off the SS2.

In the north of the region, **Lago di Bolsena** is one of Europe's largest volcanic lakes. Its main town is **Bolsena** (p40), a charming place with a hilltop medieval centre and a famous 13th-century miracle story.

To get there from Rome, take the A1 north until you reach the Orvieto turn off. You should see Bolsena signposted via the ring road around Orvieto. Get on to the SR71, which heads down towards Montefiascone, and after about 10 minutes you should see side road SR13 branching off to Bolsena.

Site, is all that remains of the formidable Etruscan city that once stood here.

Founded in the 9th century BC, Cerveteri was a powerful member of the Etruscan League, and, for a period between the 7th and 5th centuries, one of the Mediterranean's most important commercial centres.

◉ Sights

Necropoli di Banditaccia   ARCHAEOLOGICAL SITE
See p42

Museo Nazionale di Cervteri   MUSEUM
See p42

✕ Eating

Antica Locanda le Ginestre   REGIONAL ITALIAN €€
(☑06 994 33 65; www.anticalocandaleginestre.com; Piazza Santa Maria 5; fixed-price menus €20 30, meals €40-45; ⊗12.30-2.30pm & 7.30-10.30pm Tue-Sun) On a delightful *centro storico* piazza, this family-run restaurant is a top choice for quality regional food. Dishes such as risotto with asparagus tips and saffron are prepared with seasonal local produce and served in an elegant dining room and flower-filled courtyard. Book ahead.

ⓘ Information

Tourist Information Point (☑06 9955 2637; Piazza Aldo Moro; ⊗9.30am-12.30pm Mon-Sat, 10am-1pm Sun winter, 9.30am-12.30pm & 4-6pm spring, 9.30am-12.30pm & 5.30-7.30pm summer) Kiosk by the entrance to the historic centre.

ⓘ Getting There & Around

Take either Via Aurelia (SS1) or the Civitavecchia autostrada (A12) and exit at Cerveteri–Ladispoli.

Tarquinia

POP 16,480 / ELEV 169M

Some 90km northwest of Rome, Tarquinia is the pick of Lazio's Etruscan towns. The highlight is the magnificent Unesco-listed necropolis and its extraordinary frescoed tombs, but there's also a fantastic Etruscan museum (the best outside of Rome) and an atmospheric medieval centre.

◉ Sights

Necropoli di Monterozzi   ARCHAEOLOGICAL SITE
See p42

Museo Archeologico Nazionale Tarquiniense   MUSEUM
See p42

🛏 Sleeping & Eating

Camere Del Re   HOTEL €
(☑0766 85 58 31; www.cameredelre.com; Via San Pancrazio 41; s €55-70, d €69-120, q €99-129; ❄🤶) Just off the historic centre's main strip, this quiet hotel has 10 spacious rooms decorated in simple, monastic style with vaulted ceilings, wrought-iron bedsteads and the occasional fresco.

Il Cavatappi   ITALIAN €€
(☑0766 84 23 03; www.cavatappirestaurant.it; Via dei Granari 2; meals €30; ⊗7.30-9.45pm Wed-Mon, 12.30-2pm Fri-Sun, longer hrs summer) Tarquinia has several decent eateries, including this family-run restaurant in the *centro storico*. It specialises in traditional regional dishes, so expect cheese and local salamis, flavoursome grilled meats and *acquacotta*, a soup thickened with bread and vegetables.

ℹ Information

Tourist Office (☎ 0766 84 92 82; www.tar quiniaturismo.it; Barriera San Giusto; ☺9am-12.30pm & 4-7pm) In the town's medieval gate (Barriera San Giusto).

ℹ Getting There

Take the autostrada for Civitavecchia and then Via Aurelia (SS1).

Viterbo

POP 66,560 / ELEV 327M

The largest town in northern Lazio, Viterbo is a much overlooked gem with a handsome medieval centre and a relaxed, provincial atmosphere.

Founded by the Etruscans and later taken over by the Romans, it developed into an important medieval centre, and in the 13th century became the seat of the popes. It was bombed heavily in WWII, but much of its historic core survived and is today in remarkably good nick. This, together with its good bus connections, makes it a pleasant base for exploring Lazio's rugged north.

◎ Sights

Palazzo dei Priori HISTORIC BUILDING
(entrance Via Ascenzi 1 Mon-Fri, Piazza del Plebiscito 14 Sat & Sun; ☺9am-1pm & 3-6.30pm Mon-Fri, 9am-noon & 4-7pm Sat, 9am-noon Sun) **FREE** Viterbo's 15th-century city hall dominates Piazza del Plebiscito, the elegant Renaissance square that has long been the city's political and social hub. It's not all open to the public but

you can visit a series of impressively decorated halls whose 16th-century frescoes colourfully depict Viterbo's ancient origins.

Outside, the elegant courtyard and fountain were added two centuries after the *palazzo* was completed in the late 1400s.

Cattedrale di San Lorenzo CATHEDRAL
(Piazza San Lorenzo; ☺10am-1pm & 3-7pm Tue-Sun, to 6pm winter) With its landmark black-and-white bell tower, Viterbo's 12th-century *duomo* looms over Piazza San Lorenzo, the religious nerve centre of the medieval city. Originally built to a simple Romanesque design, it owes its current Gothic look to a 14th-century makeover and a partial post-WWII reconstruction.

Many of its treasures are today housed in the adjacent **Museo Colle del Duomo** (☎ 320 7911328; www.museocolledelduomo.com; Piazza San Lorenzo 8; admission €3, incl guided visit to cathedral & Palazzo dei Papi €9; ☺10am-1pm & 3-7pm Tue-Sun, to 6pm winter), including a reliquary said to contain St John the Baptist's chin.

Palazzo dei Papi HISTORIC BUILDING
(☎ 320 7911328; www.museocolledelduomo.com; Piazza San Lorenzo; incl cathedral & Museo Colle del Duomo €9; ☺guided tours only) Flanking Piazza San Lorenzo, this handsome Gothic *palazzo* was built for the popes who lived in Viterbo from 1257 to 1281. To go inside you'll have to sign up for a tour at the Museo Colle del Duomo, but you can sometimes pop up the stairs to the **loggia** (colonnade) and peer into the **Sala del Conclave**, scene of the first and longest-ever papal conclave.

OFF THE BEATEN TRACK

AROROUND VITERBO

Largely overlooked by travellers, the lush, emerald-green countryside around Viterbo hides some wonderful treasures. Chief among them is **Palazzo Farnese** (☎076164 60 52; Piazza Farnese 1, Caprarola; adult/reduced €5/2.50; ☺8.30am-6.45pm Tue-Sun, garden entry 10am, 11am, noon, 3pm & 4pm Tue-Fri winter, plus 5pm summer), 20km southeast of Viterbo in Caprarola. A 16th-century Renaissance *palazzo*, it features a distinct pentagonal design and, inside, an internal circular courtyard and extraordinary columned staircase. Visits take in the richly frescoed rooms and, on weekdays, the beautiful hillside gardens.

For more horticultural splendours, head to Bagnaia and **Villa Lante** (☎0761 28 80 08; Via Jacopo Barozzi 71; adult/reduced €5/2.50; ☺8.30am-1hr before sunset Tue-Sun), whose 16th-century mannerist gardens feature monumental fountains and an ingenious water cascade.

Some 30km north of Viterbo, Bagnoregio is home to one of Lazio's most dramatic apparitions, the **Civita di Bagnoregio**, aka *il paese che muore* (the dying town). This medieval village, accessible by footbridge only, sits atop a huge stack of slowly crumbling rock in a dramatic deep-cut valley.

The story goes that in 1271, three years after the death of Clemente IV, the college of cardinals still hadn't elected a successor. To encourage them in their deliberations, the Viterbesi locked the dithering priests in the turreted *sala* and fed them nothing but bread and water until they eventually elected Pope Gregory X.

Chiesa di Santa Maria Nuova   CHURCH
(Piazza Santa Maria Nuova; ⊙ church 7am-7pm, cloisters 10am-noon & 4-7pm) This 11th-century Romanesque church, the oldest in Viterbo, was restored to its original form after sustaining bomb damage in WWII. Traces of 13th-century frescoes line the solemn, grey interior, whilst outside you can see a stone pulpit where St Thomas Aquinas preached in 1266. Also of note is the church's cloister, the so-called **Chiostro Longobardo**.

Museo Nazionale Etrusco   MUSEUM
(⌨ 0761 32 59 29; Piazza della Rocca; adult/reduced €6/3; ⊙ 8.30am-7.30pm Tue-Sun) Housed in the Albornaz fortress, this modest museum is the place for a shot of ancient culture. Reconstructions and locally found artefacts illustrate the Etruscan lifestyle, while a series of life-sized statues hark back to the city's Roman past.

🛏 Sleeping

Medieval House   B&B €
(⌨ 393 4501586; www.bbmedievalhouse.com; Via Sant'Andrea 78; s €40-60, d €60-110; 🕸 🛜) Run by the gregarious Matteo, this welcoming B&B near the medieval walls makes for a wonderful base – it's within easy walking distance of all the main sights but is far enough out to offer a quiet night's sleep. The look is exposed brick and homey furniture, and breakfast is a feast of *cornetti* (croissants) and cured meats.

Tuscia Hotel   HOTEL €
(⌨ 0761 34 44 00; www.tusciahotel.com; Via Cairoli 41; s €40-64, d €62-82; 🕸 🛜) The best of the city's central hotels, this business-like three-star has large and light rooms in a convenient and easy-to-find location. There's also a sunny roof terrace and parking (€8). Note that not all rooms have air-con.

🍴 Eating & Drinking

Al Vecchio Orologio   OSTERIA, PIZZA €€
(⌨ 335 337754; www.alvecchioorologio.it; Via dell'Orologio Vecchio 25; meals €30, pizzas €6.50-8; ⊙ 7.30-10.30pm daily & 12.30-2.30pm Sat & Sun) This much-lauded eatery hits the bullseye with its charming location – in a vaulted *centro storico palazzo* – and excellent local cuisine. There's a full range of pizzas but to get the best out of the kitchen, opt for the main menu and dishes like ricotta and asparagus tortelloni with saffron, speck and radicchio, and lamb glazed with balsamic vinegar.

Ristorante Tre Re   TRATTORIA €€
(⌨ 0761 30 46 19; Via Gattesco 3; meals €30; ⊙ 12.30-2.30pm & 7.30-10pm Fri-Wed) Viterbo's oldest trattoria is a cosy spot for steaming plates of seasonally driven dishes and earthy specialities such as *pollo alla viterbese*, roast chicken with spiced potato and olives.

Magnamagna   WINE BAR
(Vicolo dei Pellegrini 2; ⊙ 12.30-3pm & 6.30pm-1am, closed Mon & Tue lunch) Join the 30-something crowd for a glass of wine in the atmospheric setting of Piazza della Morte. The bar, which also serves craft beers and local foodie specialities, is standing room only, but there's seating outside in the piazza and in a vaulted hall known as the Winter Garden, where you can kick back to jazz gigs and DJ sets.

ℹ Information

Tourist Office (⌨ 0761 32 59 92; Via Filippo Ascenzi 4; ⊙ 9am-1pm & 2.30-3pm Mon, 10am-1pm & 3-7pm Tue-Sun)

ℹ Getting There & Away

Viterbo is about a 1½-hour drive up Via Cassia (SS2). Once in town, the best bet for parking is either Piazza Martiri d'Ungheria or Piazza della Rocca.

ROAD TRIP ESSENTIALS

Italy
Driving Guide

Italy's stunning natural scenery, comprehensive road network and passion for cars makes it a wonderful road-trip destination.

Driving Fast Facts

➜ **Right or left?** Drive on the right
➜ **Manual or automatic?** Mostly manual
➜ **Legal driving age** 18
➜ **Top speed limit** 130km/h to 150km/h (on autostradas)
➜ **Signature car** Flaming red Ferrari or Fiat 500

DRIVING LICENCE & DOCUMENTS

When driving in Italy you are required to carry with you:
➜ The vehicle registration document
➜ Your driving licence
➜ Proof of third-party liability insurance

Driving Licence

➜ All EU member states' driving licences are fully recognised throughout Europe.
➜ Travellers from other countries should obtain an International Driving Permit (IDP) through their national automobile association. This should be carried with your licence; it is not a substitute for it.
➜ No licence is needed to ride a scooter under 50cc. To ride a motorcycle or scooter up to 125cc, you'll need a licence (a car licence will do). For motorcycles over 125cc you need a motorcycle licence.

INSURANCE

➜ Third-party liability insurance is mandatory for all vehicles in Italy, including cars brought in from abroad.
➜ If driving an EU-registered vehicle, your home country insurance is sufficient. Ask your insurer for a European Accident Statement (EAS) form, which can simplify matters in the event of an accident.
➜ Hire agencies provide the minimum legal insurance, but you can supplement it if you choose.

HIRING A CAR

Car-hire agencies are widespread in Italy but pre-booking on the internet is often cheaper. Considerations before renting:
➜ Bear in mind that a car is generally more hassle than it's worth in cities, so only hire one for the time you'll be on the open road.
➜ Consider vehicle size carefully. High fuel prices, extremely narrow streets and tight parking conditions mean that smaller is often better.
➜ Road signs can be iffy in remote areas, so consider booking and paying for satnav.

Standard regulations:
➜ Many agencies have a minimum rental age of 25 and a maximum of 79. You can sometimes hire if you're over 21 but supplements will apply.

→ To rent you'll need a credit card, valid driver's licence (with IDP if necessary) and passport or photo ID. Note that some companies require that you've had your licence for at least a year.

→ Hire cars come with the minimum legal insurance, which you can supplement by purchasing additional coverage.

→ Check with your credit-card company to see if it offers a Collision Damage Waiver, which covers you for additional damage if you use that card to pay for the car.

The following are among the most competitive multinational and Italian car-hire agencies.

Avis (☑199 100133; www.avis.com)

Budget (☑800 4723325; www.budget.com)

Europcar (☑199 307030; www.europcar.com)

Hertz (☑199 112211; www.hertz.com)

Italy by Car (☑091 639 31 20; www.italyby car.it) Partners with Thrifty.

Maggiore (☑199 151120; www.maggiore.it) Partners with Alamo and National.

MOTORCYCLES

Agencies throughout Italy rent motorbikes, ranging from small Vespas to larger touring bikes. Prices start at around €80/400 per day/week for a 650cc motorcycle.

BRINGING YOUR OWN VEHICLE

There are no major obstacles to driving your own vehicle into Italy. But you will have to adjust your car's headlights if it's a left-hand-drive UK model. You'll need to carry the following in the car:

→ A warning triangle

→ A fluorescent reflective vest to wear if you have to stop on a major road

→ Snow chains if travelling in mountainous areas between 15 October and 15 April

MAPS

We recommend you purchase a good road map for your trip. The best driving maps are produced by the **Touring Club Italiano** (www.touringclub.com), Italy's largest map publisher. They are available at bookstores across Italy or online at the following:

Stanfords (www.stanfords.co.uk)

Omni Resources (www.omnimap.com)

ROADS & CONDITIONS

Italy's extensive road network covers the entire peninsula and with enough patience you'll be able to get just about anywhere. Road quality varies – the autostradas are generally excellent but smaller roads, particularly in rural areas, are not always great. Heavy rain can cause axle-busting potholes to form and road surfaces to crumble.

Local Expert: Driving Tips

A representative of the Automobile Club d'Italia (ACI) offers these pearls to ease your way on Italian roads:

→ Pay particular attention to the weather. In summer when it gets very hot, always carry a bottle of water with you and have some fresh fruit to eat. Italy is a sunny country but, in winter, watch out for ice, snow and fog.

→ On the extra-urban roads and autostradas, cars have to have their headlights on even during the day.

→ Watch out for signs at the autostrada toll booths – the lanes marked 'Telepass' are for cars that pay through an automatic electronic system without stopping.

→ Watch out in the cities – big and small – for the Limited Traffic Zones (ZTL) and pay parking. There is no universal system for indicating these or their hours.

Coins

Always try to keep some coins to hand. They come in very useful for parking meters.

Traffic in and around the main cities is bad during morning and evening rush hours. Coastal roads get very busy on summer weekends. As a rule, traffic is quietest between 2pm and 4pm.

Road Categories

Autostradas Italy boasts an extensive network of autostradas, represented on road signs by a white 'A' followed by a number on a green background. The main north–south link is the Autostrada del Sole (the 'Motorway of the Sun'), which runs from Milan (Milano) to Reggio di Calabria. It's called the A1 from Milan to Rome (Roma), the A2 from Rome to Naples (Napoli), and the A3 from Naples to Reggio di Calabria. There are tolls on most motorways, payable by cash or credit card as you exit. To calculate the toll price for any given journey, use the route planner on www.autostrade.it.

Strade statali State highways; represented on maps by 'S' or 'SS'. Vary from four-lane highways to two-lane main roads. The latter can be extremely slow, especially in mountainous regions.

Strade regionali Regional highways connecting small villages. Coded 'SR' or 'R'.

Strade provinciali Provincial highways; coded 'SP' or 'P'.

Strade locali Often not even paved or mapped.

Along with their A or SS number, some Italian roads are labelled with an E number – for example, the A4 autostrada is also shown as the E64 on maps and signs. This E number refers to the road's designation on the Europe-wide E-road network. E routes, which often cross national boundaries, are generally made up of major national roads strung together. The E70, for example, traverses 10 countries and includes the Italian A4, A21 and A32 autostradas, on its course from northern Spain to Georgia.

Limited Traffic Zones

Many town and city centres are off-limits to unauthorised traffic at certain times. If you drive past a sign with the wording *Zona a Traffico Limitato* you are entering a Limited Traffic Zone (ZTL) and risk being caught on camera and fined. Being in a hire car will not exempt you from this rule.

If you think your hotel might be in a ZTL, contact them beforehand to ask about access and parking arrangements.

ROAD RULES

➡ Drive on the right side of the road and overtake on the left. Unless otherwise indicated, give way to cars entering an intersection from a road on your right.

➡ Seatbelt use (front and rear) is required by law; violators are subject to an on-the-spot fine.

➡ In the event of a breakdown, a warning triangle is compulsory, as is use of an approved yellow or orange safety vest if you leave your vehicle. Recommended accessories include a first-aid kit, spare-bulb kit and fire extinguisher.

➡ Italy's blood-alcohol limit is 0.05%, and random breath tests take place. If you're involved in an accident while under the influence, the penalties can be severe.

Road-Trip Websites

AUTOMOBILE ASSOCIATIONS

Automobile Club d'Italia (www.aci.it) Has a comprehensive online guide to motoring in Italy. Provides 24-hour roadside assistance.

CONDITIONS & TRAFFIC

Autostrade (www.autostrade.it) Route planner, weather forecasts and the traffic situation in real time. Also lists service stations, petrol prices and toll costs.

MAPS

Michelin (www.viamichelin.it) Online road-trip planner.

Tutto Città (www.tuttocitta.it) Good for detailed town and city maps.

Driving Problem-Buster

I can't speak Italian, will that be a problem? When at a petrol station you might have to ask the attendant for your fill-up. The thing to do here is ask for the amount you want, so *venti euro* for €20 or *pieno* for full. And always specify *benzina senza piombo* for unleaded petrol and *gasolio* for diesel. At autostrada toll booths, the amount you owe appears on a read-out by the booth.

What should I do if my car breaks down? Call the service number of your car-hire company. The Automobile Club d'Italia (ACI) provides a 24-hour roadside emergency service – call ☎803 116 from a landline or mobile with an Italian provider or ☎800 116800 from a foreign mobile phone. Foreigners do not have to join but instead pay a per-incident fee. Note that in the event of a breakdown, a warning triangle is compulsory, as is use of an approved yellow or orange reflective vest if you leave your vehicle.

What if I have an accident? For minor accidents there's no need to call the police. Fill in an accident report – Constatazione Amichevole di Incidente (CAI; Agreed Motor Accident Statement) – through your car-hire firm or insurance company.

What should I do if I get stopped by the police? The police will want to see your passport (or photo ID), licence, car registration papers and proof of insurance.

What if I can't find anywhere to stay? Always book ahead in summer and popular holiday periods. Italy doesn't have chains of roadside motels, so if it's getting late head to the nearest town and look for signs for an *albergo* (hotel).

Will I be able to find ATMs? Some autostrada service stations have ATMs (known as *bancomat* in Italian). Otherwise, they are widely available in towns and cities.

Will I need to pay tolls in advance? No. When you join an autostrada you have to pick up a ticket at the barrier. When you exit you pay based on the distance you've covered. Pay by cash or credit card. Avoid Telepass lanes at toll stations.

Are the road signs easy to read? Most signs are fairly obvious but it helps to know that town/city centres are indicated by the word *centro* and a kind of black-and-white bullseye sign; *divieto fermata* means 'no stopping'; and *tutte le direzione* means 'all directions', i.e access to major roads or intersections.

➡ Headlights are compulsory day and night for all vehicles on autostradas and main roads.

➡ Helmets are required on all two-wheeled transport.

➡ Motorbikes can enter most restricted traffic areas in Italian cities.

➡ Speeding fines follow EU standards and are proportionate with the number of kilometres that you are caught driving over the speed limit, reaching up to €2000 with possible suspension of your driving licence. Speed limits are as follows:

Autostradas 130km/h to 150km/h
Other main highways 110km/h
Minor, non-urban roads 90km/h
Built-up areas 50km/h

Road Etiquette

➡ Italian drivers are fast, aggressive and skilful. Lane hopping and late braking are the norm and it's not uncommon to see cars tailgating at 130km/h. Don't expect cars to slow down for you or let you out. As soon as you see a gap, go for it. Italians expect the unexpected and react swiftly, but they're not used to ditherers, so be decisive.

➡ Flashing is common on the roads and has several meanings. If a car behind you flashes it means: 'Get out of the way' or 'Don't pull out, I'm not stopping'. But if an approaching car flashes you, it's warning you that there's a police check ahead.

➡ Use of the car horn is widespread. It might be a warning but it might equally be an expression of frustration at slow-moving traffic or celebration that the traffic light's turning green.

PARKING

➡ Parking is a major headache. Space is at a premium in towns and cities and Italy's traffic wardens are annoyingly efficient.

➡ Parking spaces outlined in blue are designated for paid parking – get a ticket from the nearest meter (coins only) or *tabaccaio* (tobacconist) and display it on your dashboard. Note,

however, that charges often don't apply overnight, typically between 8pm and 8am.

➡ White or yellow lines almost always indicate that residential permits are needed.

➡ Traffic police generally turn a blind eye to motorcycles or scooters parked on footpaths.

FUEL

➡ You'll find filling stations all over, but smaller ones tend to close between about 1pm and 3.30pm and on Sunday afternoons.

➡ Many have *fai da te* (self-service) pumps that you can use any time. Simply insert a bank note into the payment machine and press the number of the pump you want.

➡ Italy's petrol prices are among the highest in Europe and vary from one service station (*benzinaio, stazione di servizio*) to another. When this book was researched, lead-free petrol (*benzina senza piombo*) averaged €1.63 per litre, with diesel (*gasolio*) averaging €1.35 per litre.

Road Distances (km)

Note

Distances between Palermo and mainland towns do not take into account the ferry from Reggio di Calabria to Messina. Add an extra hour to your journey time to allow for this crossing.

	Bari	Bologna	Florence	Genoa	Milan	Naples	Palermo	Perugia	Reggio di Calabria	Rome	Siena	Trento	Trieste	Turin	Venice
Bologna	681														
Florence	784	106													
Genoa	996	285	268												
Milan	899	218	324	156											
Naples	322	640	534	758	858										
Palermo	734	1415	1345	1569	1633	811									
Perugia	612	270	164	432	488	408	1219								
Reggio di Calabria	490	1171	1101	1325	1389	567	272	816							
Rome	482	408	302	526	626	232	1043	170	664						
Siena	714	176	70	296	394	464	1275	103	867	232					
Trento	892	233	339	341	218	874	1626	459	1222	641	375				
Trieste	995	308	414	336	420	948	1689	543	1445	715	484	279			
Turin	1019	338	442	174	139	932	1743	545	1307	702	460	349	551		
Venice	806	269	265	387	284	899	799	394	1296	567	335	167	165	415	
Verona	808	141	247	282	164	781	1534	377	1139	549	293	97	250	295	120

Italy Playlist

Nessun dorma Puccini

O sole mio Traditional

Tu vuoi fare l'americano Renato Carsone

Vieni via con me Paolo Conte

That's Amore Dean Martin

Four Seasons Vivaldi

SAFETY

The main safety threat to motorists is theft. Hire cars and foreign vehicles are a target for robbers and although you're unlikely to have a problem, thefts do occur. As a general rule, always lock your car and never leave anything showing, particularly valuables, and certainly not overnight. If at all possible, avoid leaving luggage in an unattended car. It's a good idea to pay extra to leave your car in supervised car parks.

RADIO

RAI, Italy's state broadcaster, operates three national radio stations – Radio 1, 2 and 3 – offering news, current affairs, classical and commercial music, and endless phone-ins. Isoradio, another RAI station, provides regular news and traffic bulletins. There are also thousands of commercial radio stations, many broadcasting locally. Major ones include Radio Capital, good for modern hits; Radio Deejay, aimed at a younger audience; and Radio 24, which airs news and talk shows.

Italy
Travel Guide

GETTING THERE & AWAY

AIR

Italy's main international airports:

Rome Leonardo da Vinci (Fiumicino; www.adr.it) Italy's principal airport.

Rome Ciampino (www.adr.it) Hub for Ryanair flights to Rome (Roma).

Milan Malpensa (www.milanomalpensa1.eu, www.milanomalpensa2.eu) Main airport of Milan (Milano).

Milan Linate (www.milanolinate.eu) Milan's second airport.

Bergamo Orio al Serio (www.sacbo.it)

Turin (www.turin-airport.com)

Bologna Guglielmo Marconi (www.bologna-airport.it)

Pisa Galileo Galilei (www.pisa-airport.com) Main international airport for Tuscany

Venice Marco Polo (www.veniceairport.it)

Naples Capodichino (www.gesac.it)

Bari Palese (www.aeroportidipuglia.it)

Catania Fontanarossa (www.aeroporto.catania.it) Sicily's busiest airport.

Palermo Falcone-Borsellino (www.gesap.it)

Cagliari Elmas (www.sogaer.it) Main gateway for Sardinia.

Car hire is available at all of these airports.

CAR & MOTORCYCLE

Driving into Italy is fairly straightforward – thanks to the Schengen Agreement, there are no customs checks when driving in from neighbours France, Switzerland, Austria and Slovenia.

Aside from the coast roads linking Italy with France and Slovenia, border crossings into Italy mostly involve tunnels through the Alps (open year-round) or mountain passes (seasonally closed or requiring snow chains). The list below outlines the major points of entry.

Austria From Innsbruck to Bolzano via A22/E45 (Brenner Pass); Villach to Tarvisio via A23/E55.

France From Nice to Ventimiglia via A10/E80; Modane to Turin (Torino) via A32/E70 (Fréjus Tunnel); Chamonix to Courmayeur via A5/E25 (Mont Blanc Tunnel).

Slovenia From Sežana to Trieste via SS58/E70.

Switzerland From Martigny to Aosta via SS27/E27 (Grand St Bernard Tunnel); Lugano to Como via A9/E35.

SEA

International car ferries sail to Italy from Albania, Croatia, Greece, Malta, Montenegro, Morocco, Slovenia, Spain and Tunisia. Some routes only operate in summer, when ticket prices rise. Prices for vehicles vary according to their size. Car hire is not always available at ports, so check beforehand on the nearest agency.

The website www.traghettionline.com (in Italian) details all of the ferry companies in the Mediterranean. The principal operators serving Italy:

Agoudimos Lines (www.agoudimos.it) Greece to Bari (11 to 16 hours) and Brindisi (seven to 14 hours).

Endeavor Lines (www.endeavor-lines.com) Greece to Brindisi (seven to 14 hours).

Grandi Navi Veloci (www.gnv.it) Barcelona to Genoa (18 hours).

Jadrolinija (www.jadrolinija.hr) Croatia to Ancona (from nine hours) and Bari (10 hours).

Practicalities

➡ **Smoking** Banned in all closed public spaces.

➡ **Time** Italy uses the 24-hour clock and is on Central European Time, one hour ahead of GMT/UTC.

➡ **TV & DVD** The main TV channels: state-run RAI-1, RAI-2 and RAI-3; Canale 5, Italia 1 and Rete 4; and La 7. Italian DVDs are regionally coded 2.

➡ **Weights & Measures** Italy uses the metric system, so kilometres not miles, litres not gallons.

Minoan Lines (www.minoan.gr) Greece to Venice (22 to 30 hours) and Ancona (16 to 22 hours).

Montenegro Lines (www.montenegrolines. net) Bar to Bari (nine hours).

Superfast (www.superfast.com) Greece to Bari (11 to 16 hours) and Ancona (16 to 22 hours).

Ventouris (www.ventouris.gr) Albania to Bari (eight hours).

TRAIN

Regular trains on two western lines connect Italy with France (one along the coast and the other from Turin into the French Alps). Trains from Milan head north into Switzerland and on towards the Benelux countries. Further east, two lines connect with Central and Eastern Europe.

Trenitalia (www.trenitalia.com) offers various train and car-hire packages that allow you to save on hire charges when you book a train ticket – see the website for details.

DIRECTORY A–Z

ACCOMMODATION

From dreamy villas to chic boutique hotels, historic hideaways and ravishing farmstays, Italy offers accommodation to suit every taste and budget.

Seasons & Rates

➡ Hotel rates fluctuate enormously from high to low season, and even from day to day depending on demand, season and booking method (online, through an agency etc).

➡ As a rule, peak rates apply at Easter, in summer and over the Christmas/New Year period. But there are exceptions – in the mountains, high season means the ski season (December to late March). Also, August is high season on the coast but low season in many cities where hotels offer discounts.

➡ Southern Italy is generally cheaper than the north.

Reservations

➡ Always book ahead in peak season, even if it's only for the first night or two.

➡ In the off-season, it always pays to call ahead to check that your hotel is open. Many coastal hotels close for winter, typically opening from late March to late October.

➡ Hotels usually require that reservations be confirmed with a credit-card number. No-shows will be docked a night's accommodation.

B&Bs

B&Bs can be found throughout the country in both urban and rural settings. Options include restored farmhouses, city *palazzi* (mansions), seaside bungalows and rooms in family houses. Prices vary but as a rule B&Bs are often better value than hotels in the same category. Note that breakfast in an Italian B&B will often be a continental combination of bread rolls, croissants, ham and cheese. For more information, contact **Bed & Breakfast Italia** (www.bbitalia.it).

Hotels & Pensioni

A *pensione* is a small, family-run hotel or guesthouse. Hotels are bigger and more expensive than *pensioni*, although at the cheaper end of the market, there's often little difference between the two. All hotels are rated from one to five stars, although this rating relates to facilities only and

Sleeping Price Ranges

The price ranges listed in this book refer to a double room with bathroom.

€ less than €100

€€ €100–€200

€€€ more than €200

gives no indication of value, comfort, atmosphere or friendliness.

Breakfast in cheaper hotels is rarely worth setting the alarm for. If you have the option, save your money and pop into a bar for a coffee and *cornetto* (croissant).

➡ One-star hotels and *pensioni* tend to be basic and often do not offer private bathrooms.

➡ Two-star places are similar but rooms will generally have a private bathroom.

➡ Three-star hotel rooms will come with a hairdryer, minibar (or fridge), safe and air-con. Many will also have satellite TV and wi-fi.

➡ Four- and five-star hotels offer facilities such as room service, laundry and dry-cleaning.

Agriturismi

From rustic country houses to luxurious estates and fully functioning farms, Italian farmstays, known as *agriturismi* (singular – *agriturismo*) are hugely popular. Comfort levels, facilities and prices vary accordingly but the best will offer swimming pools and top-class accommodation. Many also operate restaurants specialising in traditional local cuisine.

Agriturismi have long thrived in Tuscany and Umbria, but you'll now find them across the country. For listings and further details, check out the following sites:

Agriturismo.com (www.agriturismo.com)

Agriturismo.it (www.agriturismo.it)

Agriturismo-Italia.net (www.agriturismo-italia.net)

Agriturismo.net (www.agriturismo.net)

Agriturismo Vero (www.agriturismovero.com)

Agriturist (www.agriturist.com)

Other Options

Camping A popular summer option. Most campsites are big, summer-only complexes with swimming pools, restaurants and supermarkets. Many have space for RVs and offer bungalows or simple, self-contained flats. Minimum stays sometimes apply in high season. Check out www.campeggi.com and www.camping.it.

Hostels Hostels around the country offer dorm beds and private rooms. Breakfast is usually included in rates and dinner is sometimes available for about €10. For listings and further details, see www.aighostels.com or www.hostelworld.com.

Book Your Stay Online

For more accommodation reviews by Lonely Planet authors, check out http://hotels.lonelyplanet.com/italy. You'll find independent reviews, as well as recommendations on the best places to stay. Best of all, you can book online.

Convents & Monasteries Some convents and monasteries provide basic accommodation. Expect curfews, few frills and value for money. Useful resources include www.monasterystays.com, www.initaly.com/agri/convents.htm and www.santasusanna.org/comingToRome/convents.html.

Refuges Mountain huts kitted out with bunk rooms sleeping anything from two to a dozen or more people. Many offer half-board (bed, breakfast and dinner) and most are open from mid-June to mid-September.

Villas Villas and *fattorie* (farmhouses) can be rented in their entirety or sometimes by the room. Many have swimming pools.

ELECTRICITY

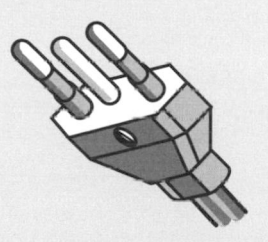

230V/50Hz

120V/60Hz

FOOD

A full Italian meal consists of an antipasto (appetiser), *primo* (first course, usually a pasta, risotto or polenta), *secondo* (second course, meat or fish) with *contorno* (vegetable side dish) or *insalata* (salad), and *dolce* (dessert) and/or fruit. When eating out it's perfectly OK to mix and match and order, say, a *primo* followed by an *insalata* or *contorno*.

Where to Eat

Trattorias Traditional, often family-run eateries offering simple, local food and wine. Some newer-wave trattorias offer more creative fare and scholarly wine lists. Generally cheap to midrange in price.

Eating Price Ranges

The following price ranges refer to a meal consisting of a *primo* (first course), *secondo* (second course), *dolce* (dessert) and a glass of house wine for one:

€ less than €25

€€ €25–€45

€€€ more than €45

Restaurants More formal, and more expensive, than trattorias, with more choice and smarter service. Reservations are generally required for popular and top-end places.

Pizzerias Alongside pizza, many pizzerias also offer antipasti, pastas, meat and vegetable dishes. They're often only open in the evening. The best have a wood-oven *(forno a legna)*.

Bars & Cafes Italians often breakfast on *cornetti* and coffee at a bar or cafe. Many bars and cafes sell *panini* (bread rolls with simple fillings) at lunchtime and serve a hot and cold buffet during the early evening *aperitivo* (aperitif) hour.

Wine Bars At an *enoteca* (plural – *enoteche*) you can drink wine by the glass and eat snacks such as cheeses, cold meats, bruschette and *crostini* (little toasts). Some also serve hot dishes.

Markets Most towns and cities have morning produce markets where you can stock up on picnic provisions. Villages might have a weekly market.

GAY & LESBIAN TRAVELLERS

➡ Homosexuality is legal in Italy and well tolerated in the major cities. However, overt displays of affection by homosexual couples could attract a negative response, particularly in the more conservative south and in smaller towns.

➡ There are gay clubs in Rome, Milan and Bologna, and a handful in places such as Florence (Firenze). Some coastal towns and resorts (such as Viareggio in Tuscany and Taormina in Sicily) see much more action in summer.

Useful resources:

Arcigay & Arcilesbica (www.arcigay.it) Bologna-based national organisation for gays and lesbians.

GayFriendlyItaly.com (www.gayfriendly italy.com) English-language site produced by Gay.it, with information on everything from hotels to homophobia issues and the law.

Gay.it (www.gay.it) Website listing gay bars and hotels across the country.

Pride (www.prideonline.it) National monthly magazine of art, music, politics and gay culture.

HEALTH

➡ Italy has a public health system that is legally bound to provide emergency care to everyone.

➡ EU nationals are entitled to reduced-cost, sometimes free, medical care with a European Health Insurance Card (EHIC), available from your home health authority.

➡ Non-EU citizens should take out medical insurance.

➡ For emergency treatment, you can go to the *pronto soccorso* (casualty) section of an *ospedale* (public hospital), though be prepared for a long wait.

➡ Pharmacists can give advice and sell over-the-counter medication for minor illnesses. Pharmacies generally keep the same hours as other shops, closing at night and on Sundays. A handful remain open on a rotation basis (*farmacie di turno*) for emergency purposes. These are usually listed in newspapers. Closed pharmacies display a list of the nearest ones open.

➡ In major cities you are likely to find English-speaking doctors or a translator service available.

➡ Italian tap water is fine to drink.

➡ No vaccinations are required for travel to Italy.

INTERNET ACCESS

➡ An increasing number of hotels, B&Bs, hostels and even *agriturismi* offer free wi-fi. You'll also find it in many bars and cafes.

➡ The 🛜 icon used throughout this book indicates wi-fi is available.

➡ Rome and Bologna are among the cities that provide free wi-fi, although you'll have to register for the service at www.romawireless.com (Rome) and www.comune.bologna.it/wireless (Bologna) and have an Italian mobile phone number.

➡ Venice (Venezia) offers pay-for wi-fi packages online at www.veniceconnected.com.

➡ Internet access is not as widespread in rural and southern Italy as in urban and northern areas.

➡ Internet cafes are thin on the ground. Typical charges range from €2 to €6 per hour. They might require formal photo ID.

➡ Many top-end hotels charge upwards of €10 per day for access.

Italian Wine Classifications

Italian wines are classified according to strict quality-control standards and carry one of four denominations:

DOCG (Denominazione di Origine Controllata e Garantita) Italy's best wines; made in specific areas according to stringent production rules.

DOC (Denominazione di Origine Controllata) Quality wines produced in defined regional areas.

IGT (Indicazione geografica tipica) Wines typical of a certain region.

VdT (Vino da Tavola) Wines for everyday drinking; often served as house wine in trattorias.

MONEY

Italy uses the euro. Euro notes come in denominations of €500, €200, €100, €50, €20, €10 and €5; coins come in denominations of €2 and €1, and 50, 20, 10, five, two and one cents.

For the latest exchange rates, check out www.xe.com.

Admission Prices

➡ There are no hard and fast rules, but many state museums and galleries offer discounted admission to EU seniors and students.

➡ Typically, EU citizens under 18 and over 65 enter free and those aged between 18 and 24 pay a reduced rate.

➡ EU teachers might also qualify for concessions. In all cases you'll need photo ID to claim reduced entry.

ATMs

ATMs (known as *bancomat*) are widely available throughout Italy and are the best way to obtain local currency.

Credit Cards

➡ International credit and debit cards can be used in any ATM displaying the appropriate sign. Visa and MasterCard are among the most widely recognised, but others such as Cirrus and Maestro are also well covered.

Tipping Guide

Taxis Round the fare up to the nearest euro.

Restaurants Many locals don't tip waiters, but most visitors leave 10% if there's no service charge.

Cafes Leave a coin (as little as €0.10 is acceptable) if you drank your coffee at the counter, or 10% if you sat at a table.

Hotels Bellhops usually expect €1 to €2 per bag; it's not necessary to tip the concierge, cleaners or front-desk staff.

➡ Only some banks give cash advances over the counter, so you're better off using ATMs.

➡ Cards are good for paying in most hotels, restaurants, shops, supermarkets and toll booths. Some cheaper *pensioni*, trattorias and pizzerias only accept cash. Don't rely on credit cards at museums or galleries.

➡ Check any charges with your bank. Most banks now build a fee of around 2.75% into every foreign transaction. Also, ATM withdrawals can attract a further fee, usually around 1.5%.

➡ In an emergency, call to have your card blocked:

Amex (☑06 7290 0347 or your national call number)

Diners Club (☑800 393939)

MasterCard (☑800 870866)

Visa (☑800 819014)

Moneychangers

You can change money in banks, at post offices or at a *cambio* (exchange office). Post offices and banks tend to offer the best rates; exchange offices keep longer hours, but watch for high commissions and inferior rates.

OPENING HOURS

Banks 8.30am to 1.30pm and 2.45pm to 4.30pm Monday to Friday.

Bars & Cafes 7.30am to 8pm, sometimes until 1am or 2am.

Clubs 10pm to 4am.

Post Offices Main offices 8am to 7pm Monday to Friday, 8.30am to noon Saturday; branches 8am to 2pm weekdays, 8.30am to noon Saturday.

Restaurants Noon to 3pm and 7.30pm to 11pm; sometimes later in summer and in the south. Kitchens often shut an hour earlier than final closing time; most places close at least one day a week.

Shops 9am to 1pm and 3.30pm to 7.30pm (or 4pm to 8pm) weekdays. In larger cities, department stores and supermarkets typically open 9am to 7.30pm or 10am to 8pm Monday to Saturday, some also on Sunday.

PUBLIC HOLIDAYS

Individual towns have public holidays to celebrate the feasts of their patron saints. National public holidays:

Capodanno (New Year's Day) 1 January

Epifania (Epiphany) 6 January

Pasquetta (Easter Monday) March/April

Giorno della Liberazione (Liberation Day) 25 April

Festa del Lavoro (Labour Day) 1 May

Festa della Repubblica (Republic Day) 2 June

Festa dei Santi Pietro e Paolo (Feast of St Peter & St Paul) 29 June

Ferragosto (Feast of the Assumption) 15 August

Festa di Ognisanti (All Saints' Day) 1 November

Festa dell'Immacolata Concezione (Feast of the Immaculate Conception) 8 December

Natale (Christmas Day) 25 December

Festa di Santo Stefano (Boxing Day) 26 December

SAFE TRAVEL

Italy is a relatively safe country but petty theft can be a problem. There's no need for paranoia but be aware that thieves and pickpockets operate in touristy areas, so watch out when exploring the sights in Rome, Florence, Venice, Naples etc.

Be sure to lock your doors – cars, particularly those with foreign number plates or rental-company stickers, provide rich pickings for thieves.

In case of theft or loss, report the incident to the police within 24 hours and ask for a statement. Some tips:

➡ Keep essentials in a money belt but carry your day's spending money in a separate wallet.

➡ Wear your bag/camera strap across your body and away from the road – thieves on mopeds can swipe a bag and be gone in seconds.

➡ Never drape your bag over an empty chair at a street-side cafe or put it where you can't see it.

➡ Always check your change to see you haven't been short changed.

- - - - - - - - - - - - - - - - - - - -

TELEPHONE

Domestic Calls

➡ Italian telephone area codes all begin with 0 and consist of up to four digits. Area codes are an integral part of all Italian phone numbers and must be dialled even when calling locally.

➡ Mobile-phone numbers are nine or 10 digits and have a three-digit prefix starting with a 3.

➡ Toll-free (free-phone) numbers are known as *numeri verdi* and usually start with 800.

➡ Non-geographical numbers start with 840, 841, 848, 892, 899, 163, 166 or 199. Some six-digit national rate numbers are also in use (such as those for Alitalia, rail and postal information).

International Calls

➡ To call Italy from abroad, call the international access number (☑011 in the USA, ☑00 from most other countries), Italy's country code (☑39) and then the area code of the location you want, including the leading 0.

➡ The cheapest options for calling internationally are free or low-cost computer programs such as Skype, cut-rate call centres and international calling cards.

➡ Cut-price call centres can be found in all of the main cities, and rates can be considerably lower than from Telecom payphones.

➡ Another alternative is to use a direct-dialling service such as AT&T's USA Direct (access number ☑800 172444) or Telstra's Australia Direct (access number ☑800 172610), which allows you to make a reverse-charge (collect) call at home-country rates.

➡ To make a reverse-charge international call from a public telephone, dial ☑170.

Mobile Phones (Cell Phones)

➡ Italy uses GSM 900/1800, which is compatible with the rest of Europe and Australia but not with North American GSM 1900 or the totally different Japanese system.

➡ Most smart phones are multiband, meaning that they are compatible with a variety of international networks. Check with your service provider to make sure it is compatible and beware of calls being routed internationally (very expensive for a 'local' call). In many cases you're better off buying an Italian phone or unlocking your phone for use with an Italian SIM card.

➡ If you have a GSM multiband phone that you can unlock, it can cost as little as €10 to activate a prepaid SIM card in Italy. **TIM** (Telecom Italia Mobile; www.tim.it), **Wind** (www.wind.it) and **Vodafone** (www.vodafone.it) offer SIM cards and have retail outlets across Italy. You'll usually need your passport to open an account.

➡ Once you're set up with a SIM card, you can easily purchase recharge cards (allowing you to top up your account with extra minutes) at tobacconists and news stands, as well as some bars, supermarkets and banks.

Payphones & Phonecards

➡ You'll find payphones on the streets, in train stations and in Telecom offices. Most accept only *carte/schede telefoniche* (phonecards), although some accept credit cards.

➡ Telecom offers a range of prepaid cards; for a full list, see www.telecomitalia.it/telefono/carte-telefoniche.

➡ You can buy phonecards at post offices, tobacconists and news stands.

Important Numbers
- - - - - - - - - - - - - - - - - -

Italy country code (☑39)

International access code (☑00)

Police (☑113)

Carabinieri (military police; ☑112)

Ambulance (☑118)

Fire (☑115)

Roadside assistance (☑803 116 from a landline or mobile with an Italian provider; ☑800 116800 from a foreign mobile phone)

TOILETS

➡ Public toilets are thin on the ground in Italy. You'll find them in autostrada service stations (generally free) and in main train stations (usually with a small fee of between €0.50 and €1).

➡ Often, the best thing is to nip into a cafe or bar, although you'll probably have to order a quick drink first.

➡ Keep some tissues to hand as loo paper is rare.

TOURIST INFORMATION

Practically every village, town and city in Italy has a tourist office of sorts. These operate under a variety of names: Azienda di Promozione Turistica (APT), Azienda Autonoma di Soggiorno e Turismo (AAST), Informazione e Assistenza ai Turisti (IAT) and Pro Loco. All deal directly with the public and most will respond to written and telephone requests for information.

Tourist offices can usually provide a city map, lists of hotels and information on the major sights. In larger towns and major tourist areas, English is usually spoken.

Main offices are generally open Monday to Friday; some also open on weekends, especially in urban areas and in peak summer season. Info booths (at train stations, for example) may keep slightly different hours.

Tourist Authorities

The **Italian National Tourist Office** (ENIT; www.enit.it) maintains international offices. See the website for contact details.

Regional tourist authorities are more concerned with planning, marketing and promotion than with offering a public information service. However, they offer useful websites, such as:

Emilia-Romagna (www.emiliaromagna turismo.it)

Lazio (www.ilmiolazio.it)

Tuscany (www.turismo.intoscana.it)

Umbria (www.regioneumbria.eu)

Veneto (www.veneto.to)

Other useful websites include www.italia.it and www.easy-italia.com.

TRAVELLERS WITH DISABILITIES

Italy is not an easy country for travellers with disabilities. Cobbled streets, blocked pavements and tiny lifts cause problems for wheelchair users. Not a lot has been done to make life easier for the deaf or blind, either.

A handful of cities publish general guides on accessibility, among them Bologna, Milan, Padua (Padova), Reggio Emilia, Turin, Venice and Verona. Contact the relevant tourist authorities for further information. Other helpful resources:

Handy Turismo (www.handyturismo.it) Information on Rome.

Milano per Tutti (www.milanopertutti.it) Covers Milan.

Lonely Planet's free Accessible Travel guide can be downloaded here: http://lptravel.to/AccessibleTravel.

Useful organisations:

Accessible Italy (www.accessibleitaly.com) Specialises in holiday services for travellers with disabilities. This is the best first port of call.

Consorzio Cooperative Integrate (www.coinsociale.it) This Rome-based organisation provides information on the capital (including transport and access) and is happy to share its contacts throughout Italy. Its **Presidio del Lazio** (www.presidiolazio.it) program seeks to improve access for tourists with disabilities.

Tourism for All (www.tourismforall.org.uk) This UK-based group has information on hotels with access for guests with disabilities, where to hire equipment and tour operators dealing with travellers with disabilities.

VISAS

➡ EU citizens do not need a visa for Italy.

➡ Residents of 28 non-EU countries, including Australia, Brazil, Canada, Israel, Japan, New Zealand and the USA, do not require visas for tourist visits of up to 90 days.

➡ Italy is one of the 15 signatories of the Schengen Convention. The standard tourist visa for a Schengen country is valid for 90 days. You must apply for it in your country of residence and you cannot apply for more than two in any 12-month period. They are not renewable within Italy.

➡ For full details of Italy's visa requirements check www.esteri.it/visti/home_eng.asp.

Language

Italian sounds can all be found in English. If you read our coloured pronunciation guides as if they were English, you'll be understood. Note that ai is pronounced as in 'aisle', ay as in 'say', ow as in 'how', dz as the 'ds' in 'lids', and that r is strong and rolled. If the consonant is written as a double letter, it's pronounced a little stronger, eg *sonno son·*no (sleep) versus *sono so·*no (I am). The stressed syllables are indicated with italics.

BASICS

Hello.	*Buongiorno.*	bwon·*jor*·no
Goodbye.	*Arrivederci.*	a·ree·ve·*der*·chee
Yes./No.	*Sì./No.*	see/no
Excuse me.	*Mi scusi.*	mee *skoo*·zee
Sorry.	*Mi dispiace.*	mee dees·*pya*·che
Please.	*Per favore.*	per fa·*vo*·re
Thank you.	*Grazie.*	*gra*·tsye

You're welcome.
Prego.   *pre*·go

Do you speak English?
Parli inglese?   *par*·lee een·*gle*·ze

I don't understand.
Non capisco.   non ka·*pee*·sko

How much is this?
Quanto costa questo?   *kwan*·to *kos*·ta *kwe*·sto

ACCOMMODATION

Do you have a room?
Avete una camera?   a·*ve*·te oo·na *ka*·me·ra

How much is it per night/person?
Quanto costa per   *kwan*·to *kos*·ta per
una notte/persona?   oo·na *no*·te/per·*so*·na

DIRECTIONS

Where's ...?
Dov'è ...?   do·*ve* ...

Can you show me (on the map)?
Può mostrarmi   pwo mos·*trar*·mee
(sulla pianta)?   (*soo*·la *pyan*·ta)

EATING & DRINKING

What would you recommend?
Cosa mi consiglia?   *ko*·za mee kon·*see*·lya

I'd like ..., please.
Vorrei ..., per favore.   vo·*ray* ... per fa·*vo*·re

I don't eat (meat).
Non mangio (carne).   non *man*·jo (*kar*·ne)

Please bring the bill.
Mi porta il conto,   mee *por*·ta eel *kon*·to
per favore?   per fa·*vo*·re

EMERGENCIES

Help!
Aiuto!   a·*yoo*·to

I'm lost.
Mi sono perso/a. (m/f)   mee *so*·no *per*·so/a

I'm ill.
Mi sento male.   mee *sen*·to *ma*·le

Call the police!
Chiami la polizia!   *kya*·mee la po·lee·*tsee*·a

Call a doctor!
Chiami un medico!   *kya*·mee oon *me*·dee·ko

Want More?

For in-depth language information and handy phrases, check out Lonely Planet's *Italian Phrasebook*. You'll find it at **shop.lonelyplanet.com**, or you can buy Lonely Planet's iPhone phrasebooks at the Apple App Store.

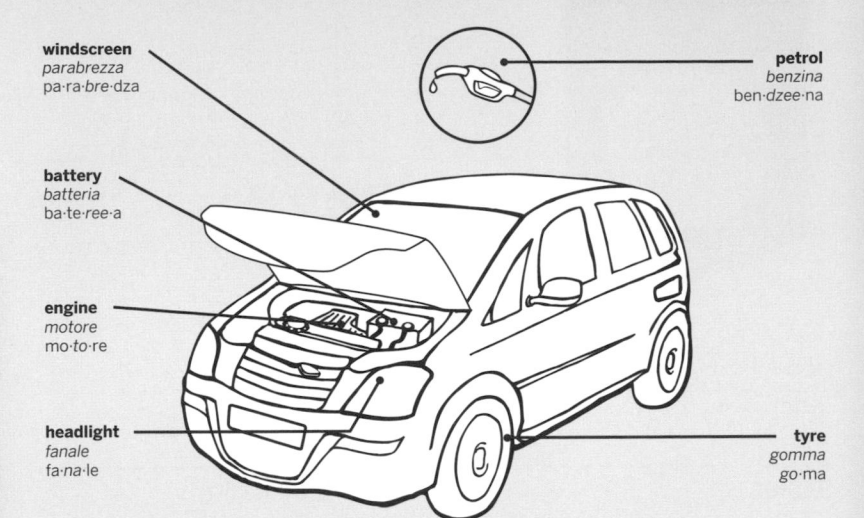

windscreen
parabrezza
pa·ra·*bre*·dza

petrol
benzina
ben·dzee·na

battery
batteria
ba·te·*ree*·a

engine
motore
mo·to·re

headlight
fanale
fa·*na*·le

tyre
gomma
go·ma

ON THE ROAD

I'd like to hire a/an ...	*Vorrei noleggiare ...*	vo·ray no·le·*ja*·re ...
4WD	*un fuoristrada*	oon fwo·ree·*stra*·da
automatic/ manual	*una macchina automatica/ manuale*	oo·na ma·*kee*·na ow·to·ma·tee·ka/ ma·noo·a·le
motorbike	*una moto*	oo·na mo·to

How much is it ...?	*Quanto costa ...?*	*kwan*·to *kos*·ta ...
daily	*al giorno*	al *jor*·no
weekly	*alla settimana*	a·la se·tee·*ma*·na

Does that include insurance?
E' compresa l'assicurazione? e kom·*pre*·sa la·see·koo·ra·*tsyo*·ne

Signs

Alt	Stop
Dare la Precedenza	Give Way
Deviazione	Detour
Divieto di Accesso	No Entry
Entrata	Entrance
Pedaggio	Toll
Senso Unico	One Way
Uscita	Exit

Does that include mileage?
E' compreso il chilometraggio? e kom·*pre*·so eel kee·lo·me·*tra*·jo

What's the city/country speed limit?
Qual' è il limite di velocità in città/campagna? kwa·le eel *lee*·mee·te dee ve·lo·chee·*ta* een chee·*ta*/kam·*pa*·nya

Is this the road to (Venice)?
Questa strada porta a (Venezia)? kwe·sta *stra*·da *por*·ta a (ve·*ne*·tsya)

(How long) Can I park here?
(Per quanto tempo) Posso parcheggiare qui? (per *kwan*·to *tem*·po) po·so par·ke·*ja*·re kwee

Where's a service station?
Dov'è una stazione di servizio? do·ve oo·na sta·*tsyo*·ne dee ser·*vee*·tsyo

Please fill it up.
Il pieno, per favore. eel *pye*·no per fa·*vo*·re

I'd like (30) litres.
Vorrei (trenta) litri. vo·ray (*tren*·ta) *lee*·tree

Please check the oil/water.
Può controllare l'olio/ l'acqua, per favore? pwo kon·tro·*la*·re lo·lyo/ la·kwa per fa·*vo*·re

I need a mechanic.
Ho bisogno di un meccanico. o bee·zo·nyo dee oon me·*ka*·nee·ko

The car/motorbike has broken down.
La macchina/moto si è guastata. la ma·kee·na/mo·to see e gwas·*ta*·ta

I had an accident.
Ho avuto un incidente. o a·*voo*·to oon een·chee·*den*·te

BEHIND THE SCENES

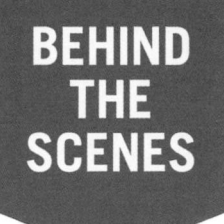

SEND US YOUR FEEDBACK

We love to hear from travellers – your comments help make our books better. We read every word, and we guarantee that your feedback goes straight to the authors. Visit **lonelyplanet. com/contact** to submit your updates and suggestions.

Note: We may edit, reproduce and incorporate your comments in Lonely Planet products such as guidebooks, websites and digital products, so let us know if you don't want your comments reproduced or your name acknowledged. For a copy of our privacy policy visit lonelyplanet.com/privacy.

ACKNOWLEDGMENTS

Climate map data adapted from Peel MC, Finlayson BL & McMahon TA (2007) 'Updated World Map of the Köppen-Geiger Climate Classification', *Hydrology and Earth System Sciences*, 11, 163344

Cover photographs

Front: Tuscany landscape, Borut Trdina/Getty

Back: Leaning Tower of Pisa, Maurizio Rellini/4Corners

THIS BOOK

This 1st edition of *Tuscany Road Trips* was researched and written by Duncan Garwood, Paula Hardy, Robert Landon and Nicola Williams This guidebook was produced by the following:

Destination Editor Anna Tyler

Product Editor Vicky Smith

Senior Cartographers Anthony Phelan, Valentina Kremenchutskaya

Book Designers Michael Buick, Katherine Marsh

Assisting Editors Jodie Martire, Kate Mathews

Assisting Book Designer Kerrianne Jenkins

Cover Researcher Naomi Parker

Thanks to Joel Cotterell, Brendan Dempsey, Grace Dobell, Kirsten Rawlings, Angela Tinson, Tony Wheeler

OUR STORY

A beat-up old car, a few dollars in the pocket and a sense of adventure. In 1972 that's all Tony and Maureen Wheeler needed for the trip of a lifetime – across Europe and Asia overland to Australia. It took several months, and at the end – broke but inspired – they sat at their kitchen table writing and stapling together their first travel guide, *Across Asia on the Cheap*. Within a week they'd sold 1500 copies. Lonely Planet was born.

Today, Lonely Planet has offices in Franklin, London, Melbourne, Oakland, Beijing and Delhi, with more than 600 staff and writers. We share Tony's belief that 'a great guidebook should do three things: inform, educate and amuse'.

INDEX

000 Map pages

NOTES

OUR WRITERS

DUNCAN GARWOOD

A Brit travel writer based in the Castelli Romani hills just outside Rome, Duncan has clocked up endless kilometres walking around the Italian capital and exploring the far-flung reaches of the surrounding Lazio region. He's co-author of the Rome city guide and has worked on the past six editions of the Italy guide as well as guides to Piedmont, Sicily, Sardinia, and Naples and the Amalfi Coast. He has also written on Italy for newspapers and magazines.

PAULA HARDY

From Lido beaches to annual Biennales and spritz-fuelled aperitivo bars, Paula has contributed to Lonely Planet Italian guides for over 15 years, including previous editions of *Venice & the Veneto, Pocket Milan, The Italian Lakes, Sicily, Sardinia* and *Puglia & Basilicata*. When she's not scooting around the bel paese, she writes for a variety of travel publications and websites. Currently she divides her time between London, Italy and Morocco, and tweets her finds @paula6hardy.

ROBERT LANDON

Ten minutes into his maiden voyage to Italy, Robert was pickpocketed in a Florence church, yet he has been returning obsessively ever since, including stints living in Rome and Florence. He has authored Lonely Planet guides to *Florence, Venice* and *Brazil*, and has also written about travel, art and architecture for the *Los Angeles Times, Dwell, Metropolis* and many other publications.

NICOLA WILLIAMS

British writer Nicola Williams lives on the southern shore of Lake Geneva. Thankfully for her Italianate soul, it is an easy hop through the Mont Blanc Tunnel to Italy where she has spent years eating her way around and revelling in its extraordinary art, architecture, cuisine and landscape. Hunting Tuscan white truffles in October is an annual family ritual. Nicola has worked on numerous titles for Lonely Planet, including those covering Italy, Milan, Turin & Genoa, and Piedmont. She shares her travels on Twitter @Tripalong.

Published by Lonely Planet Publications Pty Ltd
ABN 36 005 607 983
1st edition – Jul 2016
ISBN 978 1 76034 054 4
© Lonely Planet 2016   Photographs © as indicated 2016
10 9 8 7 6 5 4 3 2 1
Printed in China

Although the authors and Lonely Planet have taken all reasonable care in preparing this book, we make no warranty about the accuracy or completeness of its content and, to the maximum extent permitted, disclaim all liability arising from its use.